DIVINE PARTNERSHIP

Book Three of the God-Mind Plan for Saving Both Planet and Man

As revealed by the Brotherhood of God

To Jean K. Foster

Note to readers:

Words in italics are those of the writer, Jean K. Foster, including conversations with her spirit teacher. Words of the Brotherhood of God are printed in regular type.

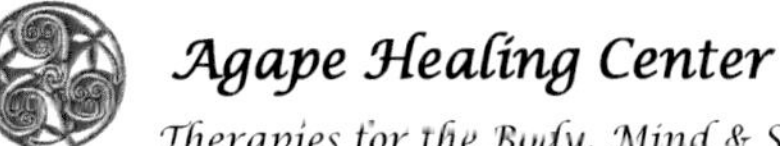

TeamUp
Box 1115
Warrensburg, MO 64093

This book is manufactured in the United States of America. Distribution by **TeamUp.** Cover design by Phil Reynolds. Jean Foster portrait by Jim Wiltse. Printing by Walsworth Publishing Company.

ISBN # 0-9626 366-1-4

Library of Congress Catalog Card Number 90- 72133

Table of Contents

DEDICATION

Because this is the final book of my two-trilogy assignment from the Brotherhood — "Trilogy of Truth" and "Truth for the New Age" — I feel it only appropriate that I write the following dedication:

For his acceptance of the truth in the two trilogies, his editorial skills, his constant encouragement and continuing financial support in the entire project, I dedicate — on behalf of the Brotherhood and myself — this concluding book, "Divine Partnership," to my earth partner, Carl B. Foster.

JEAN K. FOSTER

COMMENTS FROM THE BROTHERHOOD OF GOD

The gentle teamwork between the writer and the Brotherhood has brought this present trilogy into print. The eternal truth gives the reader hope for the New Age because it teams up with what everyone wants within his being — to present greatness (God truth that manifests as substance) into the earth plane to help the planet team up with its perfection.

To realize the totality of this three-part textbook, we who have written it through the writer now want to give you an overview of the content. The brightness of reality is spirit, of course. Those who read The Trilogy of Truth[1] already know that spirit is the eternal truth of who we are — you on the earth and we who stand nearby in our realities. Teaming up with those who open their minds is what we want to do. Presences in spirit form who unite with the realities (spirits) of those who inhabit the earth is what we open ourselves to. Those of us who team up with you and with the God of the Universe want only to bring you our help, our understanding and our perfect truth.

Because we can help each open mind / spirit to become one with God-mind, we remain nearby, the eternal partners ready to help you with the living of your life. The work of our Brotherhood is only to help you manifest in the earth plane whatever you want to manifest in the way of good. That is our charge, our purpose, our gentle nature revealed.

In the first trilogy of books — "The God-Mind Connection," "The Truth That Goes Unclaimed" and "Eternal Gold" — we established the purpose of the Brotherhood, the way to contact us, the nature of the gentle truth that comes from God-mind and the method by which you become one with understanding and one with manifestation.

Those who opened their minds to us became channels of truth and teamwork. They who gave up earth-mind truth (that which is embodied in mankind's knowledge and understanding) in order to be totally in touch with God-mind truth are now channels of truth who bring greatness into the earth plane. "Greatness" is manifesting God truth into the planet and into their lives.

The work that every Brother enters into is that of helper. But when the Brotherhood enters into communication with you, we then become teammates. No entity opens into Pure Truth from God without teamwork because the way is unclear. We who team up with those in the earth plane halt the despair, halt the pointless pursuance of old truth that was given by men, not God. The Brothers know the way to God-mind, and they lead those who want to go there.

Come, you who hone your talents in the teamwork of fellow spirits. Open your mind, open your heart, open your being to our brightness, to our understanding. We who welcome you team up with you because our assignment that comes from God is clear: "Go into the universe with this message, with this understanding — that God is more than earth truth explains. Teamwork with Me will make your life perfect. Open to this understanding."

The gentle partnership of the Brotherhood, of you in human form, and of the God of the Universe is that which will turn the planet into paradise, that which will bring pure benign productivity into your lifetime experience.

The second trilogy, **Truth for the New Age,**[2] is the textbook that will take you through and into the New

Age. What is this Age? A period of earth life that will begin with the change of polarity. Then it will go forward into the perfect planet which will bring its delights to those who live there. But to know how to survive the turmoil before the earth settles down, the student of life must open himself or herself to much new understanding.

The second trilogy through the writer we name Truth-giver is your guide to teamwork that will provide the truth, the understanding, the perfection, the protection and yes, the very substance that will meet your needs. This trilogy enters as the three books, "New Earth—New Truth," "Masters of Greatness" and "Divine Partnership." To open your mind to these three books is to provide yourself with wonderful help that will give you the means not only to survive the turmoil that will ensue, but to help you to meet all needs.

Tender truth on the matter of the New Age appears in the first book. That which must occur is explained in terms that you will recognize as true. Within "New Earth—New Truth" will be an invitation to dedicate yourself to being one of the leaders, one of the new masters of greatness. The master is one who will lead others in the Age to come, one who will understand how to manifest whatever is needed and whatever is perfect for the period. That which you will need is explained that you may go toward a specific goal.

The second book, "Masters of Greatness," eternalizes the qualities that each master must develop to be that teammate who will lead people in the New Age. This book outlines the open teamwork that will give masters their guidance. It provides the exercises that will prepare you to enact the role of master. This book opens you, the candidate for master, to the full impact of the turmoil that will occur when the earth responds to a new polarity. But this turmoil is not told to you to frighten you. It is told only to prepare you to work within the teamwork to take a leadership role in providing people with safety and provisions.

This book, "Divine Partnership," provides advanced studies only for those who have become masters. Therefore, only you who have teamed up with us to study the first two books will now understand and become open to the truths taught in this book. Those who now go forward in spirit to be one with God and to become leaders in the New Age when earth truth will no longer function will find the information they need. They will use the resources of this book with the authority of those who have committed themselves completely.

Center in the true work of spirit, readers, and team up with this trilogy. Teamwork is explained to enable you to move forward with ease. Tender understanding must be understood and applied if you are to be leaders, right? To help you become a master of greatness, we eternalize (visualize with God power) the being that you are. We eternalize you filled with truth from God-mind. Then we promise you that each step of the way is that which the Brotherhood, the God of the Universe and you take together.

Read, study, enter into each book in order. Then, when that is completed, you will, if you have done all the exercises and the experiments and entered into teamwork, become the one-with-God individual that is a master of greatness.

Gentle presences work with you when you read and study these books. They hover nearby waiting for your questions, your cry to help with understanding. Be a true partner by readying yourself to meet the coming Age with power.

[1] **Trilogy of Truth:** "The God-Mind Connection," 1987; "The Truth That Goes Unclaimed," 1987; "Eternal Gold," 1988; Jean K. Foster. **TeamUp,** Warrensburg, Missouri.

[2] **Truth for the New Age:** "New Earth — New Truth," 1988; "Masters of Greatness," 1990; "Divine Partnership," 1991; Jean K. Foster. **TeamUp,** Warrensburg, Missouri.

Upheaval of the Earth

1

The role of masters of greatness is to help others survive.

To understand what lies ahead in the New Age, readers must open their minds to the eternalization of purity, not of a holocaust. Purity is your watchword when the earth teams up with truth to receive that which will bring it to its greatness. Therefore, open your minds to what this book presents — the evolving of the earth as it leaves that which is old, that which is no longer valid, and reaches out to join itself with the Creator Who brings the teamwork of productivity.

The eternalization you hold in mind will help to bring more gentleness into the period between the old and the new. That perfect realization on your part of what is happening, what is taking place in the earth's apparent freedom from polarity will mark the difference between chaos and an open mind of cooperation.

Now join with those who bring this material through God-mind and release your fears of the events that precede the New Age. There is nothing to fear if you center in God eternalization: A visualization plus the truth which comes through God-mind. Who is your Partner? Those who have become masters of greatness[1] know that they are in partnerships that will lead them right through the period we speak of now.

They will step forth to call to those who are frightened and concerned. These masters will help people to understand what is happening, why there must be cooperation, what teamwork will do to bring the open truth into visible form.

You who are masters know that your partnership is with the Teammate Who is the Source of All that IS. To bring sense into the New Age, you must rely on the partnership completely, not the old earth truth which will be unreliable. Those who have studied the earth, analyzed it and who have given their understanding to others, have no real comprehension of what the world will be like when the New Age takes place. Therefore, if you want to bring forth order, bring the good of God into manifestation. Lay aside the old and pick up the new.

When there is no polarization, there is no understandable position upon which the earth rests. Although this eternalization we bring you is not to be permanent, it will last enough time to bring great destruction of all that responds to normal gravity. The reason we give you this explanation is to present the first need of the New Age — the need of some way to respond to a center point which will hold people in place. The earth will be turning, it will be undulating, it will be entering a new position in the heavenly scheme of the universe. Therefore, until the position is reached, people will believe there is no end in sight, no hope for a more permanent kind of earth structure.

Those who understand what is happening will know the situation is temporary, and they will offer hope to others. The masters will immediately rise to this understanding and will present the predicament to those whom they gather together. "The earth will right itself soon," the masters will say. "The earth is turning on its side, gradually and with purpose. Team up to withstand the hardships until the earth has pointed to its new polarity."

The earth in motion and without polarity will seem to be a raging cruise through dangerous waters. People will think they will capsize momentarily. They will rise and fall, their feet entering the air to move effortlessly through the wetness of despair. Those who receive the understanding that the earth is going into a change may want to move forward to the purpose of the New Age.

So that people will remain relatively calm, we suggest that all masters and all those who know that the New Age is approaching, gather people together. Bring them assurances that stability will be reached in the near future. If people can rely on this hope, they will want to survive, want to understand what is taking place, and they will remain relatively calm. When the situation improves, people will be ready to go forward with their earth lives.

Masters of greatness who have studied the first two textbooks in this series[2] will know the way things are working, and they must explain it to all who will listen and believe what they hear. Those who fight explanations must be given tenderness, but they must not impede the work the masters are to do. Waste no time in arguments with them. Hold no environmental truth before them. Turn to others who are ready to hear you, and get on with your work. The others must be cast aside in your thoughts to fend for themselves until they turn their minds to understanding.

Those who receive the words that you speak, masters of greatness, will be your nucleus to turn the earth experience into meaningful activity. Tell them that the God of the Universe — the greatness that proves the energy of creativity — will be the temporary gravity to give them stability. This temporary gravity is within the very acts they feel and experience, but God IS that center which is gravity itself. Therefore, they must turn to this God concept and realize its power in their lives. By doing this, the teamwork will provide a calm base to hold them safely in place.

Generous options will then appear to this nucleus group. They will see how the movement of the earth has a rhythm that they may use to their advantage.

Those who open to this rhythm will then be part of the teamwork of creativity, not the object of it. They will be in the midst of the rhythm, their own bodies responding to that of creativity, and they will no longer be bounced around without purpose.

Bright spirits will join you, those who enter your plane from this nearby plane. They will help you put your lives into rhythmic energy that is being used to place the earth in its new position. Then there will be no fear, only trust in the new way of things.

The masters who arrive to help you will explain all this to those who are your responsibility. People may be afraid because the earth is changing so rapidly that they no longer recognize it, but you must say to them, "Hold fast, for we are being guided just as the earth is being guided. We will arrive in the right place where we will prosper, where we will remain to live our lives."

Those who no longer question the plan will rest in the tender assurance, teaming up with the generous God plan of righting the planet into its great potential.

Be true, masters, to that commitment you made when we brought you the understanding you will need in this New Age. Hold yourself open to receive even more truth that will promote understanding among the group you have assembled. Tell them not to mourn those who have not survived, for they are now in spirit form. They are preparing to reenter earth to help attain the wonderful truth. Mourning has no place because their understanding must be centered in the truth that spirit is reality.

The way to bring wholeness to all bodies that have experienced some kind of problem, is to recognize wholeness as the truth that must manifest. Tell those who have physical problems to make way for wholeness, not to hold onto that which is not whole. Then demand they let go of inferior thought patterns based on earth truth — even in medicine or medical understanding. The greatness of truth holds all medical understanding and much more. The truth promotes the positive energy of eternal truth, and all earth knowledge must bow to what is of eternal God Truth.

Never hesitate to proclaim the God of the Universe as the energy, for the generous God Truth is certainly the Source of all energy. Therefore, when you proclaim the truth, you hold before others a proper understanding. Those who cry out that people are being punished, those who cry out that God has abandoned them, must receive new truth. Team up with no outbursts of this kind. Laugh, if you can, shake your head, pour the terrible words out upon the ground to wrest the earth power from them.

"Take such truth and depart," you must tell them. Say to them firmly, "Team up with others like yourself. **This** cluster of people only teams up with the greatness which is God, not the old earth truth of a poor God whose pleasure is to hurt and punish. Worship such a God if you must, but depart from this group!"

Be firm. Be persuasive. Those who want to hold to such beliefs will begin to fall away from the cluster because they cannot believe in the greatness of God. There will be some who begin to fall away, and then they will cry out to others to help them.

"Help yourself!" you must say firmly. "We cannot change your beliefs."

There may be a general outcry from those with tender hearts to save those who float away to their own cluster. They may urge you to do something. They may be angry toward you. Wear your master's mantle before them. Repeat the premises that will team people up with the noble purpose of the New Age. Then say to them, "I AM not God! I AM spirit and I AM body, but I AM not God. The being that I am, my spirit self, is teamed up with this great God, not to promote my own whims, but to promote the greatness which is God."

To help others understand, tell them they, too, can be masters. Remind them that they have the same abilities you have. You are not conceived as God; you are conceived just as they. Tell them to promote their good and the good of others by promoting their own understanding of Who and What God IS. Then proceed to teach them. Those who will be ready to understand will take what you say and apply it to themselves. Others will try to argue. Tell them that you have no time for arguments. Take their arguments to God. Then call those who will again commit themselves to the New Age to step forth with you. Tell them to join the cluster of people who intend to unite with God to bring great truth upon the planet and into their lives.

We cannot tell you in advance how many times you will have to ask for recommitment and give others a chance to disengage themselves. The point is that masters must serve their purpose of holding fast to the truth and not make compromises with earth truth. Those who make compromises, those who renege upon their commitments, those who turn to others' opinions will become only ordinary leaders. They will not know how to put people into the positive force of God which will see them safely through the interim period.

When the winds begin to soften, when the earth no longer undulates, when those in your care release themselves to the earth itself, you will know the ordeal is ended. The polarity will have been reached, the positive and negative forces will be in effect, and you are once again responding to gravity. Then tell the people, "God is the greatness of creativity; He is the purpose of purity; He is that spirit within the earth itself that expresses the reunion with whatever is good. The God Who is our Partner is not a petty God given to human qualities because God IS what is perfect and good. Those who respond to what is perfection will be partners with God. That is the thrust of the message I am to give you. Team up with this greatness and learn to listen to the truth that will enter your mind, thought to thought.

Team up, you masters of greatness, to help people express God Truth. Enter into their understanding. Eternalize **with** them, **not apart** from them. Then they will learn how God Truth manifests. But if you go apart to produce the truth, they will honor YOU, not GOD. Yours is the awesome task, but you will not be alone, for we in the Brotherhood of God, advanced spirits in the next plane of life, will stand among you to bring our support. Rely on our comfort, our strength, our presence as real and meaningful.

A question floated out from my mind to the mind bringing these words. "A point arises," noted the communicator, "that on the earth planet, will we (the Brotherhood) be seen?" Then came the response. "Only those who have eyes to see will see us. By this we mean that if you are entirely open to our presence, you will open your inner eyes and then your outer eyes will open also."

This entire chapter came in a burst of words, and I made no effort to stop for evaluation. Later, however, I asked about the instruction masters are to give to people about God being a "temporary gravity." Something about this statement seemed improper.

Temporary gravity is the way to present God here in the turmoil of this change. People will want gravity, not some concept to ponder. They will be afraid; they will be teamed up with all sorts of misunderstandings. But they know they need, above all else, gravity. The idea of God as gravity will hold their attention, and they will want to work for temporary gravity until the earth stabilizes.

[1] "Masters of Greatness," book two of **"Truth for the New Age,"** 1990, Jean K. Foster. **TeamUp,** Warrensburg, Missouri.

[2] "New Earth — New Truth," 1988 and "Masters of Greatness," 1990; Jean K. Foster. **TeamUp,** Warrensburg, Missouri.

Teaming up with Eternal Truth

2

How to release your potential to create what you will need in the New Age.

The Brotherhood opens this chapter with a challenge to those who have received their mantles of masters of greatness.[1]

To team up with eternal truth in the New Age you must enter into the partnership with the expectations of one who is now assured of greatness manifesting in the earth plane. There must be no wavering in attitude, nor must there be any partnership with earth-mind truth.

In earlier books we brought these points to the reader. But now we want to elaborate on this theme we have played over and over again.[2]

The first elaboration is based on the eternal truth that God IS whatever is good and great. You who read this book believe this truth with your minds and with your hearts, we are sure. But do you believe it with the part of you that enters into creativity?

The creative portion of your being, which must be ready to perform greatness in the earth plane, becomes the catalyst to manifest great truth. Whatever you create, whatever you put your mind to, must perform in the outer dimension or you will not be what people need or what we expect from you. Therefore, move toward perfect understanding of God Truth. We who assist you now enter to focus this aspect of you into the creative force of manifestation.

Enter now into the fold of those who stand ready to demonstrate. Team up with your Partner if you feel any sense of separation. Then realize that the world needs purity. It needs to be without poisons both in the earth and in the air. Turn your purification signal to "on." Then send out waves of purity within the environment in which you live. Try this now. Do not hesitate.

The atmosphere rises to meet your expectations. You who enact this experiment undoubtedly breathe more freely and with great purity. The body self improves in its cell tone, and the developing purity spreads out to all who enter your environment.

Now try another experiment. The eternal truth that we work with now is that the God of the Universe holds no thought of anger or punishment. Therefore, people are free and able to proceed with their lives. Use this truth on those you know, those who tend to bear guilt for their emotions, their feelings, for the things that others lay on their minds. Join each person to this truth, holding yourself there among them. There is no guilt because there is no condemnation! You are free! You are wonderful in the eyes of your Partner. Those whom you hold up along side the truth also feel wonderful, and they know they are free.

Be the person who knows mastery consists of that which is totally released to the Truth of God. Hold no part of yourself back; know the release that enters with this understanding.

Join with us now into yet another elaboration of the rule of masters — that God Truth must be used daily, used freely, used with great generosity. When you really comprehend this great truth, you will be busy within the partnership bringing truth into the planet and into its inhabitants.

Turn generously toward all God Truth, not just one

or two items. The pessimism that some masters may feel occurs when they do not work at their task of bringing truth to the world they know and understand. They lean back, seemingly afraid to perform, afraid to make a mistake, afraid to send the truth outward. They feel themselves in a kind of secret band that must not perform. But, why should you have such a feeling? The time to act, masters, is now.

Therefore, let us each pick a truth that we want to use freely and with generosity. This truth must emanate through the partnership you each have formed. Turn now to the Partner.

As instructed, I turned to my Partner who recently gave me the gift of wholeness to use in my world. Though I had not understood just how to use the gift, I named several people in my world as those whom I would like to give wholeness. As I named them, my Partner gave commentary. The following is an example.

"This one you name before Me is waiting to assume her wholeness, but she knows too much about religious methods to release her limited concepts. Yet, we bring her the gift of wholeness and will try to insert it between the cracks of her present armor. When she sighs in doubt of what she believes, we will insert the wholeness concept. When she breathes her prayer of releasing all to God, we will insert the wholeness concept. This person has a spirit that wants wholeness, but which accepts the role of invalid. To wrest this image from her mind, we will put the wholeness concept before her inner eyes like a banner."

On my own, I would have never thought the above, let alone said it. I see this individual as a tower of strength and courage, and no doubt she is that. But my Partner sees her spirit and the cause of her physical problems. My Partner knows how she can attain wholeness. The chapter continues.

The way to put each great truth into manifestation is to work with it daily. This is not to say you must stay on your knees pleading and bargaining. Do not plea and do not bargain, for the Partner is not susceptible to these earthly ideas. God advances, not withdraws.

You must do the same. Advance in your understanding by using the truth that God gives you to use.

The writer was given the truth that allows her to write books, but yet she wanted to become one with other truth. Therefore, her Partner has given her wholeness, that which must be given away in order to be used, that which must enter the earth plane in order to be understood as successful. Therefore, the writer must, besides write this book, work with wholeness as her gift from her Partner. Eternal truth, remember, will not stay within you unless you use it generously.

Now let us try yet another experiment. Those among you who enter into the master of greatness program must go out on the proverbial limb to bring yourself into alignment with your Partner's gentle truth. Therefore, go into the temple now where you and your Partner work together. Hold yourself ready to receive your assignment from your Partner. Be ready to use the great gift of truth you receive.

My own temple radiated with my Partner's presence. I let myself be caught up in the wonder and the expectation of our teamwork. "Eternalize your greatness," came the mind-to-mind words. "Team up with your gift of wholeness and your gift of writing the two trilogies. Now put them into the perfection of your being where they will work their miracles. You have become Wholeness in Operation! You are also Truth-giver — the one who writes My truth for the progress of truth in the earth plane. The writing is approaching its close, but your gift of wholeness is now to be your gentle truth manifested."

The Brotherhood, continued with the chapter.

The writer has found a new purpose for her lifetime. The assignment of the two trilogies is coming to a close, and though she may write other books, her purpose has now been completed — the purpose for which she came. But she has found it sad that it nears its close, that her purpose seems finished. Therefore, her Partner brings her another assignment — to use the wholeness concept to bring respite to those who open themselves to truth.

Each master has a purpose, special and intense, but he or she also has other responsibilities that come along and which must be met. We speak now of those other responsibilities.

A master of greatness does not have the luxury of working with just one individual truth. The needs of earth are so vast, and the number of masters is so small in comparison with the overall population, that masters must be able to meet every need that comes before them. Therefore, the Partner will guide you whenever you name a certain need. Then, heeding your Partner's words, you and that Power will act on behalf of the expressed need, no matter what it is.

Bring the entire truth into play whenever you walk the face of the earth. Open your eyes to the needs, and rescue those who need rescuing by working openly with your Partner. There will be others like yourself who will also work with their Partners, and greatness will manifest with the suddenness of Pure Truth that cannot be held back.

You must practice, masters, practice with your Partners to realize the vast potential of the partnerships. Then you will grow in energy, grow in enthusiasm, grow in the use of truth to meet the needs of the earth plane where you make your home. Now recognize your responsibilities on the earth plane. These responsibilities may be healing and wholeness; nourishment or shelter; opportunities of tenderness and energy; purity of mind and body, or answering the serious questions of people everywhere that must be answered if they are to move forward with purpose in their lives.

The writer wonders if what we suggest is to alleviate pain of all kinds. Eternalizations of pain go out to us in this plane because people accept concepts of pain. Therefore, they manifest pain. But that which enters as pain often has its source in something hidden. That is why you must use your Partner to help identify the need.

Work with the Partner and you will see the results

manifest. Beauty will come forth. Reassurance of powerful improvement in all truth will manifest before your eyes. You will not doubt because the only possible answer is truth manifesting.

Get into the eternalization that will effect your truth. Team up with the Partner who will guide you rightly. Then together enact the truth that fits the situation, whatever it is. If people need to manifest the truth that God is their supply, then eternalize their need being met, but do not determine the exact way it will be met. The way to do this is to team up with your Partner to bring the needed supply into the open earth plane. The Partner will know the exact supply, the entering truth that will be just what will meet the need. Together you will effect this need being met.

Though it is hard to bring such things into mind right now, the time will arrive when the manifestation will come about just as we have indicated. Team up with your Partner in all manifestations of truth. Team up to recognize the need, to offer it for entering greatness, and then stand firmly in place while the need is met. This manner of working will bring about the teamwork that will, in turn, manifest the needed material substance.

The Brotherhood then answered my unspoken question.

Yes, the explanation is logical, and it is totally in line with what you have learned in the other books.[3] Therefore, you know to reach out to its eternal truth, right? The writer notes the logic, but she admits that in an actual situation, it might be hard to stand fast when others cry out their fears.

But we say to you who are masters, do not worry about the effect that fears of other people will have on you. You will stand firmly with your Partner because you will be ready.

The way to prepare is to begin now with your special truth and bring about the needed answers by the method we have outlined. When you see truth being enacted while the earth is still calm, you will naturally turn to this method of work when the time of change is upon the earth.

Bright presences always enter to help those who work at manifestation. They stand by you, helping you to maintain the calm spirit you need and the wisdom to turn to your Partner in spite of all that others may say. They will reside with you, watch over you, bring you peace of mind in your work. Rely on those who will enter whenever you find the teamwork vague or find that it brings you uneasiness. These bright ones know the truth, have experienced what you will go through, and they will open your mind further than you might do on your own.

Now team up to enter into the future when the earth has undergone its mighty travail and finally comes to rest in a new polarity. The earth will begin to stabilize, but until it is firm once again, there is no point in trying to plant gardens or to build shelters. You will need to concentrate on each day's survival — the health of minds and bodies, the entering truth and how to use it to supply food, shelter, clothing. These needs can be met easily when the master works with the Partner.

Therefore, do not fear this sort of request, master of greatness. The way to meet the needs that are so basic is the same way that you meet any other need. Turn to your Partner and say, "Those whom I have in my care need to find shelter from the wind. Where can we lead them?" The Partner will enter the problem and point out the way. Tune in to this demonstration without alarm or worry, for shelter may be given just as wisdom or wholeness or anything else is given.

"Tell them," the Partner may say, "that I AM that shelter, and that they will find respite from the cold within my own Being." Remember, the Being that God IS is whatever is good. Therefore, when you walk to the place indicated and direct those in your care inside, you will tell them that they are in the Being that is God.

Now let us enter into the eternalization that will bring more eternal truth into the earth plane, truth that calls for greatness to be manifested as needed clothing.

What can you do with earth truth? Go to the store? Weave the blanket? Enter into trade? Plant cotton or clip wool? These things will not be possible as the New Age begins because the earth is not stable enough. Survival is enough in itself — quite enough to give you a day's work. Therefore, the ONLY way to bring forth clothes is through the manifestation of them.

Tell your Partner when people say they are cold and need more clothing. "What should I tell them?" you ask.

Put your hands out to the people and ask them to eternalize their own needs. Tell them to present into the eternal truth that God IS supply. God IS the substance itself — the very clothes that will keep them warm. Mothers may act for their children. While they are manifesting their wardrobes, team up with the Partner who may say to them, "Open your eyes to My entering worth. The clothes you need may be yours only if you believe in the method that we will use together. Team up with God. Team up with your master of greatness. Then reach out into the substance and take what is yours."

There will be great thrashing about as they gather their clothing, so finely made, so perfect for their needs. They will murmur to assure themselves of its reality, and you, with a great strong voice, will remind them that this manifestation proves again that God IS their supply. Teach them in this way to manifest whatever they need whenever they need it. They need not wait for you to assume the responsibility.

Now we bring this chapter to a close, for to enter into more examples would only be repetitious. The way to manifest truth is put before you. Those needs you now see in the earth plane may be approached in the manner we outline. Work with the principles and the law to learn the way to meet the material needs of earth with the substance that is formed by the spirit.

[1] See Chapter 18, The Graduation Chapter, in "Masters of Greatness," 1990, of the trilogy, **Truth for the New Age;** Jean K. Foster. **TeamUp,** Warrensburg, Missouri.

[2] **The Trilogy of Truth** — "The God-Mind Connection," 1987; "The Truth That Goes Unclaimed," 1987; "Eternal Gold," 1988; Jean K. Foster. **TeamUp**, Warrensburg, Missouri.

[3] **Trilogy of Truth**, 1987 and 1988; **Truth for the New Age** (a second trilogy), 1989 and 1990. Jean K. Foster, **TeamUp**, Warrensburg, Missouri.

Tapping into Universal Energy

3

You can call forth Universal Energy, the requisite for manifestation.

The message which now unfolds to you, masters of greatness, is told to powerfully project (eternalize) the energy you will need to help those who have survived into the New Age. When you tap into the energy of which we speak, that which unifies with the truth will rush to **bring truth into the physical earth plane**. Therefore, in this chapter we teach you to understand this entire teamwork, to recognize the energy, to tap into it and to bring it to bear upon the truth.

Bring to this chapter your greatest concept of God of the Universe. This concept is ever growing, ever manifesting its teamwork. To open to the energy of this universe, your own energy must be raised to the level of universal thought. This adjustment means that your bright spirit must rise in thought to the Teammate or Partner with whom you abide. To enter into this arrangement perfectly, remain calm and centered in the greatest God concept you can muster.

Then when you believe you have the greatest concept that you can project, hold it in your thoughts. This projected concept will move your present energy level to greater vibrations, greater tonal energy, better understanding of what it means to be completely teamed up with this gentle, though powerful, God.

The energy level of your spirit will rise and with it the energy of your body. You will know the release of tension and the acknowledgment of great teamwork that begins within and spreads throughout your being and into all parts of your body. Then you will be ready to call forth the universal energy to enhance or to bring about whatever it is that needs accomplishing in the New Age.

Put on your mantle of the master, the mantle that reminds you of your responsibilities, your opportunities and your obligations.[1] Then look out at the land that has steadied, that is again what can be depended upon. The polarization will be established, the teamwork of the earth, sun and moon will be set once again and the land will be in a placid state. What now?

People may look to you, or they may not. Many will have learned from you how to manifest their needs, but they will still be uncertain in this "strange" land. The feel of the air will be different — cleaner, more crisp — and it will fill their lungs with goodness. They will turn about to find familiar trees, but most will be seedlings, at best. Those who have survived will want to eternalize their own homes, their own plots of ground, their best thoughts of good. But they will need help.

What will they need? They will need the universal energy that will help them create the plants, the entering greatness of beauty and superior growth. They will want to find water, a better way to farm and to live their lives. Most will be reconciled to the New Age, and they will want you to help them create great good. This will be your obligation — to help them find the best way to proceed by using God Truth. They will need lessons on truth, lessons on eternalizations, lessons on how to bring greatness (manifested truth) into the earth plane.

There will be those who will want to depend on

others, a few who will not want to do the work of spirit for themselves. But you must heed the law, masters of greatness, which says that **each person must manifest for himself or herself.** There is no way to hold onto what others bring into being through God Truth.

The energy that enters through the universal truth is not open to those who wait to be served. No, there is no way to use this truth of God and manifest it into the earth plane unless each person eternalizes. That lesson must be understood! Therefore, it is time, once again, to let those who want to proceed by way of earth truth to do so. Those who will team up together to work with God Truth will know no boundaries, no limitations. They will flourish They will sing and laugh. They will energetically enter into each day's adventure.

Those who separate according to their beliefs in earth truth will manifest in vain, for they have chosen for themselves a way that will bring them hardships and unhappiness. Be open to what is said here, for there is no way to bring people into a safe harbor unless they sail into it on their own.

While the above material came through me, I thought of the story in Genesis about the fall of man. I asked if the New Age would be, in effect, that "Garden of Eden" all over again. Here is the answer.

The story in the Bible about the Garden of Eden offers an explanation of why mankind departed from the God Who eternalized so much good before their eyes. But the writers of Genesis only surmised that people were receiving from God all that was beautiful and good. They did not understand that man and God were really partners in the beginning. The writers thought that God was the big and powerful Entity who was given to jealousy and to the giving of great temptation to mankind. They did not understand the **total goodness** that is God!

Therefore, they told a great untruth that God sent Adam and Eve out of the garden and sentenced them to hard work. The truth of God is not condemnation, masters of greatness. Therefore, do not compare what is old (that which was given in misunderstanding) with what is new (that which opens in our present teamwork). The great God concept that you have now developed puts the old concept to shame, does it not?

Those in the New Age who expect others to do their work for them will receive nothing. The reason is not that God punishes! The reason is that in the New Age people must use God Truth to manifest goodness. Those who do not choose to abide by the law that requires everyone, even children when they reach the age of understanding, to eternalize the greatness for themselves, will need to use the hard method of scratching the soil and eating whatever they find. They will not have learned that God has provided a much better way.

Those who depart from the group must be allowed to leave without rancor, without condemnation from you or others. They may choose to return when it is clear to them what they have done in turning to earth truth. Children will certainly see that the God Truth way is superior, and they will soon wonder why anyone doubts it. They are the hope that will lead the earth into the new and wonderful teamwork with the God of the Universe. When this generation grows up and raises yet another generation, earth truth will disappear. The earth will be the paradise it was always intended to be.

Those who read this book eternalize themselves remaining in the earth plane to view this new paradise, but they know that much time must go by. Will they live through this time when generations pass? Masters of greatness must understand that they need to renew their bodies in order to live on through more than one lifetime. Therefore, be assured that it is possible to take your bodies with you into this (adjoining) plane where you can be refreshed and where you will learn much that will help you to live well in the earth plane. Many of you who read this book will decide to hold onto your bodies and (be able) to return to earth to be with those whom you brought through the turmoil. They will revere your presence, and you will give them the good news of new concepts that will push their growth to great heights.

Those who enter the New Age will want to grow into spiritual teammates with God. They will want to become the wayshowers and the optimum energizers who will provide the earth with all that will make it a perfect planet. They will be open to learning and they will be communicators with their Partners. The earth will resound with the music of harmony that arises when people work well together. The music will surround the planet and unify those who reach out to be in contact with others.

The planet will be sparsely populated in the beginning, for there will be great earth turmoil. Those whose bodies died will be clamoring for a chance to return to earth to help in the work. However, there must be great spiritual growth before they return, or they will team up with thoughts of the old ways that led to the turmoil. We must work with those who departed their bodies in such great numbers and help them to forge new thoughts, new concepts, new ideals.

The greatness of God will be the power we use to wrest away all negative truth that people have held. This same power will also generate the energy that will help you in the earth plane. It will help you to align yourself with that which will team up with the greatness of God. Here is how it will work.

The God of the Universe will give His energy into the substance that is eternal and invisible to earth eyes. This energy will draw the substance into it, much as a potter uses clay. Then the power will mold that which you call forth, but you do not have to actually be a potter. The way to mold substance is to team up with the optimum energy of your own being which is merged into that of your Partner's. Then the substance will begin to mold or to call forth the object or the condition that is wanted and needed.

To those who have not read "New Earth—New Truth" and "Masters of Greatness,"[2] this procedure may seem ludicrous. But to those who have become masters, it will make sense. The way to place greatness into manifestation is to work within your Partnership. **There is no other way.**

Go forth into the earth plane that seems so stable to you today. The trees are upright. The winds are normal. The plants grow. The buildings are erect. The world seems as it has been, right? But when you stand there looking about, leaning against a tree, perhaps, team up with God to reveal to you what the New Age will be like. Then with your mind centered in God — in your Partner's Being — let the truth unfold to you.

Though we can tell you many things, you must see it for yourself. The experience must unfold through your mind, it must go forth through your own senses. Then you will be ready to understand your role when the earth produces change.

The way to handle this experience is to put your own energy into the open channel and then wait to connect with those who will unveil the future. This can be done now, or you can wait.

I meditated upon the open channel and waited a while before there was any action. The words came to "Team up," and in thought pictures, I flattened myself against the ground. I gathered my two dogs to me either because they were afraid or I was afraid for them. But there was no storm, no menacing clouds or lightning. There was only wind, and the wind came from above me straight down. It was strong enough to hold me in place, and this was good because the earth gravity began to weaken. The foundations of buildings began to shift, and then the buildings crumbled. The bricks, cement, wood — everything —crumbled straight down into the earth. The wind held me tightly against the earth, and I was told to call out to others to form a human chain that would maintain contact among us.

The earth then began to undulate like ocean waves. No longer was I lying flat on the ground. I, and others who joined in making a human chain, hovered above the earth.

We watched it until the movement ceased. Even the wind ceased at times, and we were on the ground, but we were not held there tightly. We had time to rest, to get food, to discuss what was happening. I was told what to say to others, how to reassure them.

Those who began to whimper and to let their fears get the better of them were to be told — by me — to make their own group, for this group wanted no whimpering. I mentally cringed, but the words and the strength to say them came to me. Ways to survive were offered to us, and I was told to keep up the hopes of others, for the time would come when we could all expect to live safely again upon the earth.

Water covered the land for awhile. I had the definite idea that water did not cover the entire earth, but it covered the earth below us. We who gathered together and held hands floated above the water until the water receded and again there was land. I was to dispense truth with abundant generosity.

Was I afraid? No! But I was busy! There was no time to weep or to cry over the past or to grieve for those who were not with us. The dogs vanished from sight, but I had no fears for them nor any thoughts that they were hurt or lost. In fact, my thought was that all was going according to plan. My job was to hold fast to what I knew was God Truth.

Someone from the Brotherhood commented on my visionary experience.

The writer's experience was not as clear as we would have liked it to be. This entity has the firm conviction that the entire earth change will team up only with those who want to serve the New Age, and she is not sure she wants to live through this time. However, we still believe she must prepare to serve.

Again turn your mind to the energy that you must know how to use. The optimum energy within you is your own spirit / mind that is ready to pour forth whatever it sees as good. This optimum energy alone will begin the procedure, but alone it will not pour forth God's greatness upon the earth. Therefore, pour your optimum energy into the Partnership, into the union between you and the great God Who enters your temple to be one with your being. When your energy has poured into this Partnership, the Partner will bring forth the eternal truth that God is indeed all powerful. Then you will see the wholeness that you want manifested. Then you will see certain material things that mean the body will survive.

I halted the transmission to ask a question. "When you say 'the body will survive,' do you mean it will survive this unstable period?" The Brotherhood patiently responded.

Survival means that you will be able to enter the New Age with your body whole. To enter the New Age with a weakened body is not desirable, is it? Therefore, work now to make your body strong. We eternalize that wonderful body that you will need, and we want you, with your Partner, to eternalize the body self that will best cope with the coming turmoil.

Work with the Partnership and try out what we tell you. First, team up with your Partner if you, at this time, feel any separation. Then with the certain knowledge that you and God are One, give your maximum energy to this union. Hold it within you to eternalize the union of the Partnership. This sort of thing must be done whenever you think of God as separate from you. The way to be One is to promote Oneness!

You must act within the Partnership. Now is the time to be the partner who brings greatness into being by using the Partnership. Work with this energy in all things you see. If nothing happens, then use the Partnership to question why. That Partner will give you the reason. No master of greatness will be denied the opportunity to learn his craft!

Yes, the opportunity is given you now to learn how to bring greatness into manifestation. Enter into the Partnership and pull forth the substance into the earth plane!

No one will know how to eternalize unless he or she has practiced it many times. And, when you learn to do this easily, you will be able to teach others. Even now, before the New Age, you can teach anyone who wants to know. Turn to God Truth now. Do not wait until **after** the New Age has begun.

A question bothered me. "What about people who want me to prove this power? There are many who will not try any of what you are explaining unless I — or someone they know — show them proof they can accept." The Brotherhood quickly responded.

Those who wait to receive proof will be waiting until the New Age has brought them into its turmoil. They will still be saying, "Just give me one example!" But you do not answer them, masters of greatness. They wait for you to act, instead of acting for themselves.

They think if you really do understand how to survive, then all they need do is stay close to you. But they think amiss. The way to survival is the way to eternalization! God Truth provides the means, not earth truth, and as long as some need proof, they are still aligned with earth truth. Nothing you do will turn them away from what is of earth. The weight of proof is **not** on you, or on those who demonstrate. The weight of proof is upon those who turn to earth truth as the answer to mankind's problems.

I interrupted to comment on the subject of proof and those who demand it. Since I have been writing the books that are my assignment, people have asked me to prove, in one way or another, that what comes through me is really entering through an open channel provided by the Brotherhood of God. There has been doubt about the reality of the source. There has been wonderment that seeks proof by asking questions that I, in turn, am to ask the Brotherhood.

That which the writer has given is now turned back to us for commentary. We who team up with Pure Truth to bring you these books know that there is no way she can prove anything to those who insist on entertaining their doubts. But so it is with earth truth. They want the writer or some other person to stand before their eyes and turn water into wine. But Jesus did this act, and even this seeming miracle did not persuade many, did it? No, there is no way to give proof to another. Do not even try. Each person must turn to the Partnership, work with this Partner, and turn completely to God Truth!

Your optimum energy — that which teams up with God — is the way to manifest greatness. The way to nothingness is to use your optimum energy to try to push things forward on your own. Then you end up as the entity who ridicules the truth!

Be assured that we stand behind you as you reach out individually to prove your Partnerships! To prove Partnerships is quite different from proving things to one another. The Partnership stands ready to be used, to work in the earth realm, and it only awaits your own gentle acceptance.

We began by telling you that you can tap into this optimum energy, and now we have said that you must put it into the Partnership. Do you understand what we tell you here? The Partner must have your total allegiance, your total union. Therefore, every thought, every bit of energy you have must be thrust into the Partnership which will perform the greatness.

The writer is thinking that we want you to do nothing on your own, and that is what we tell you. There is no power when you stand out there alone. There is only desire, perhaps compassion, and there may be the generous thought of helping others. But there will be no power until you thrust it all into the Partnership where the real force resides.

[1] Chapter 18, pp. 178-188, "Masters of Greatness," 1990; Jean K. Foster, **TeamUp**, Warrensburg, Missouri.

[2] "New Earth - New Truth," 1989; "Masters of Greatness," 1990; from the trilogy **Truth for the New Age**, Jean K. Foster; **TeamUp**, Warrensburg, Missouri.

Generous Eternalizations Fill All Needs

4

Jesus, the Brother of Brothers, describes how he learned to manifest while on earth.

Advanced teaching concerning eternalizations and bringing them into earth substance will challenge, comfort and delight you. In this chapter, the Brother of Brothers speaks frankly and lovingly about his life on earth, and he offers his own experience in Israel as proof of how a Partnership with God results in the manifestation of truth into earth forms.

The Brotherhood begins the chapter.

To learn how to satisfy all needs, generously apply the principles and the law of God. With a generous belief in the teamwork of the Partnership, whatever people want and need will be manifested in the age to come. Teamwork is the key, of course, not just an entity within an earth plane body who sends his request to God.

Enter into the teaching which will open everything that may seem hidden. We bring you an explanation of what teamwork actually does in the earth plane. To understand what is given, hold your mind wide open, open to the truth.

The one we think of as perfect in demonstration will bring you this next part of the chapter. He is that Brother of Brothers who now opens himself to the reader to make it clear what the "miracles" consist of in reality. This individual takes on his cloak of the earth figure who entered life to enact truth. This individual enters with full remembrance of what life in the earth plane was like, and now he offers his own explanation of how his mastery came about.

Team up, ye masters of greatness! Team up all those who search for something more than earth truth. Team up to learn for yourselves how greatness manifests and how it was done in that land where the Hebrews made their home.

Message from the Brother of Brothers

Those who introduce me to you call me the Brother of Brothers, but I am, for now, that one who came to earth when the kingdom of the Israelites was under the rule of Rome. I remember the people, the neighbors, my eternal truth rising within me, those who thought to direct my life — my mother and father.

Those who surrounded me hated the rule of Rome, for Rome had no thought of the great God that we, the Hebrew people, held up to praise and worship. Romans had their own beliefs, of course, and with those beliefs came certain spiritual manifestations. But we who were Hebrew felt the authority of Rome weighing upon us mightily.

My birth was not spectacular. The birth was in Bethlehem, and it was without incident. But soon after my birth, while my mother fed me from her breast, there came some to our lodging to tell us of the strange star that appeared above the city. The wisest teachers thought it was a sign that Rome would not rule us forever, but that the star of David would rise again.

There were some who wanted no part of the rabbis' teachings, for they were sure that the star meant that a new leader had been born. Those who told this story pointed to me, the oldest male child born to Joseph and Mary, to say that perhaps he might lead the Hebrews to victory over Rome. Then others came to reinforce that idea, and soon it was decided that the male child born on that night of the rising star would be the one to be the new king.

Those who perpetuated the idea thought I was the perfect rallying point for their protest against Rome — a baby, innocent and pure, the kind of symbol that would be perfect for the God fearing people of Israel. Purity — that was the thought, not that I would be that king. But the ideas were bringing much trouble for those who were my mother and father. They crouched in fear, but in a dream my father found the answer to his fears. He took us stealthily out of Bethlehem and into a foreign land.

Those who used us as symbols had their day in the notoriety of their statements, but they did not have to pay the price. They claimed that it was a revelation, and even the Romans believed that revelations are something to pay attention to. That is why they brought about the massacre.[1]

There I was, growing up without the understanding of how my father came to flee the land of my birth. The truth finally was revealed to me when my father was told that we could safely return home — this time to the place of our forefathers, Nazareth.

I tell you these things to prepare you for the rest of the message. Those who may have thought I came as God would not be impressed with "miracles," would they? They would think that, of course, God must perform miracles. Those who now know that my birth occurred even as their births occurred, must know that I came to be an expression of truth in this earth plane. I came to that land where people held the God concept of the mighty but terrible God who loved, but who also punished without respite. Here was my charge — to present the God whom I came to know. This God is the embodiment of true love, like a gentle father, not a tyrant who rules with awesome authority.

Tenderness is the concept I came to generate concerning the God of the Universe. The rest of the story — my birth, my teaching, my death — arises from the need of mankind to fill out the details with awesome information that would cause others to respect the person that I was on earth. But they lost the true thought — that it is God whom we must give our thought to, not those who happily fulfill their contracts to bring truth into the earth plane.

Here is how I began my ministry. In Nazareth I had an unquenchable need to know about God and all that God had done with the Hebrew people. Those who taught me thought I should study with the masters of the day, and this was made possible by my parents. They hoped I might be a rabbi, one who is respected among the people. The one who was my father, however, thought I should be able to make a living. Therefore, he taught me his trade.

There is a fact I must report here. I did not care about carpentry. There are books that picture me as a happy worker, but I must tell you that I was not eternally grateful to be working with Joseph. He was a serious task master, however, and he gave me much to accomplish. I, on the other hand, wanted to study, to contemplate, to become seriously entered into the partnership with God, whom I called "My Father." Therefore, I had to accomplish my carpentry tasks with quickness to enable me to do other things.

I would sigh and think of the box or the chest or the table that I was to work on. My earthly father would describe the work I was to do, and I could, with my inner eyes, visualize the completed work. Then I held it up to my heavenly Father and told Him that I must bring this object into manifestation in order to be about my other work. The One who joined me in the carpentry center there in Nazareth entered His Being into my own, and together we placed the Truth into creation. The Truth is, you see, God is the Partner who puts power into our projects. What I learned was that God not only inspired me, but He even brought the object into manifestation.

The writer wonders if I was surprised the first time it happened. The truth did not surprise me, nor did the manifestation, for I wanted so much for it to come about. What I had yet to learn was that the manifestation was to be given generously to all who needed help. But at first, I merely worked with my own projects. The carpentry tasks were completed so fast that my earthly father stood amazed, and he told others, "This son gives the work his best and even more."

My mother came to watch me work, and unknown to me, she saw the manifestation process in action. This one, the gentle woman who trusted her greatest concept of God, knew that I was tied into some kind of special understanding with the One Who led His people from Egypt. This mother kept all that she saw into her own mind, and she shared none of this, for she knew all too well what notoriety can do to people.

But when our family had other needs, my mother called upon me to help, and I did. The more I worked with the greatness God generously supplied, the more this greatness wanted to be expressed. That is the way it goes. The generous application of God Truth into the earth plane results in even greater truth, even greater power flowing right through the spirit and into the body.

The way to begin, those who have not yet manifested truth into the visible, is to choose something you really care about, not something that is of indifferent interest to you. I really cared that the carpentry projects be completed, and I exercised my own great energy that was already tied into the God concept with which I lived my life. The fact that I was very young helped me to thrust truth into the project, but within each of you is that same thinking. An old body does not house an old spirit. Throw aside earth truth and speculate upon the spirit within you. That youngster who wants his oneness with God to show forth enters into great energy in the matter of manifestation! The result is the same as it would be if you were young in body.

While you think about what I have already said, let me give you a brief thought process that I used while on earth in the form of Jesus of Nazareth. The thought that appeared full blown to me, whether of my own inclination or of another's, teamed up with what I wanted above all else. Was it more wine at the wedding? Well, to tell the truth, it was not. But to please my mother I would have turned myself inside out. The one who was my mother asked me to bring forth wine, and I did. She was pleased, not inordinately proud of my accomplishment! She merely was pleased her son cared to help those who were his relatives. The thought was generous, not self-serving.

And so it must be with you! The thought you send out to manifest truth must not be self-serving or given only to impress others, or it will fail in its purpose! Why? Because the Partnership must enact the truth, not you on your own. When God is taken into account, will the manifestation be done to impress others? No! Will it be given in order to secure riches? Riches are too self-serving! Then team up with your Partner and He will help you to know how earth responds to truth.

Eternalizations team up with you of needed rain, needed food for the hungry, needed shelter for the homeless. To bring about manifestation, however, team up with those who need food, shelter, or that which will remove their suffering. Only then will you truly know what meets their real needs. Only then will you be generously motivated. Involvement with others is essential if you are to help meet their needs.

Now let us each take something that we care about beyond all other things. Team up with that thought. Team up with that understanding. Then hold it into yourself. To wrest any selfishness from the thought, enter it without truth. State it. Is it open to others? If not, team up with another thought. That which comes to be given to others is the generous thought. Now that you have the thought in mind, hold it out to your Partner Who is the Power that moves mountains! The way to move mountains is to give the method, the positive thrust of your own energy to your Partner. This enforces the teamwork that brings a positive visualization that produces the pure substance of the earth. That which you hold in mind, that which is generous, that which is perfectly teamed up with your Partner must appear in the earth plane.

Now to simplify it all. The thought of true generosity is now given to God who is truly the Partner you count on. The very essence of greatness penetrates the thought and forces it into the open.

The writer visualizes the books being printed, leaving the warehouse and going forth into the waiting hands of thousands of people who want Pure Truth. This means much to her because of her own involvement in the writing. The thought is generous, and it is this truth that gives her life meaning. The thought must jell into better open truth, however. She must take her thought and permanently endow it with substance. There on her shelf are the books she has written to bring God Truth into the earth plane. She sees these books, holds them in her hands, gives them to her friends, holds no thought of entering personal gain. The work of accomplishment, then, is now given to her Partner.

For those of you who hold out generous thoughts that you want to see manifested in the earth plane, send those thoughts to your Partner. This great One accepts your thoughts and teams up with them. Hear, oh hear, ye who walk the path of masters, the truth that enters. The writer heard her truth that God IS that truth that people want and need; therefore, all who yearn to have truth will be satisfied. God meets every need, and He will meet the need for truth.

The writer may take this truth and put it into earth substance as the energy that will thrust the books into the earth realm. That is her eternalization, her manifestation. That you read this book now is evidence of her eternalization.

There will be some who seek manifestation of the earthly plunder such as gold, or the money that they may need to get them out of indebtedness. They will enter this money into God Truth that says, God IS my supply; my every need is satisfied. Then they put the truth, not the visualization of money, into their own situation. Gathering the wherewithal will be very satisfying and will release the fears of teaming up with earth substance.

That which opens to you as the need you must respond to, that which opens to you as the problem that you and your Partner can easily solve, this is what you must generously give your attention to. The Partnership is in place, and you must now open to that which turns energy into earth substance.

I asked the Brother of Brothers, "Is it all right to practice manifestation principles on small things?"

There will be no small thing when it comes to manifestation. Practice on big things, if you wish. The energy I used when I was a boy excited me and wanted to prove itself in the earth plane. But my reason for manifestation was not just to practice, it was to reach my goal of attaining time to study. Therefore, the things I wanted were to help provide time to further my own development spiritually. Those things that my earthly father wanted to teach me were easy for my heavenly Father to accomplish. The one named Joseph did not understand what was happening, but he always stood by me with love in his heart.

Now I stand by with love in my heart for you who reach out to manifest that which the good and generous Father gives. Why hesitate? That which I have done you can also do. That which I entered into is possible for you, too, to enter into. That is my message, my presentation — that you may reach forth without timidity, without guile and without thoughts of selfish identity to perform the seeming "miracles" that anyone can perform with his Partner.

[1] [Matthew 2:16] "Then Herod, when he saw that he had been tricked by the wise men, was in a furious rage, and he sent and killed all the male children in Bethlehem and in all that region who were two years old and under. . . . ."

Pure Truth Delivers Whatever You Designate

5

How to bring all truth into the visible earth plane where people will recognize it.

The words "Pure Truth" designate that which God-mind gives to those who seek the Source of Wisdom. This truth is the "eternal gold"[1] that people can use to bring whatever is needed into manifestation. Though this subject has been introduced and explored in their other books, master teachers now address the readers at a post graduate level.

The eternal gold of the earth plane is exactly what it seems to be — both ethereal and earth substance. The very name implies the cooperation of these two entities — truth that is of universal and spiritual value plus the material wealth of the earth itself. When you think of Pure Truth in this way, you will then rise in understanding to conquer the earth limitations which you impose upon yourself.

There may be some among you who do not need this chapter. Perhaps you are already able, as Jesus explained, to team up with your Partner to meet the needs of the earth. By "meeting the needs of the earth," we mean answering those requests, spoken and unspoken, that must be met to give life its best. If you do not need this chapter, pass over it.

The first point we must cover is the way you view the partnership. If you are still of the opinion that this partnership is only of the ethereal and not the practical, then you are not making full use of this association. That which offers itself to you — that is, the partnership — is meant to be examined closely and put to use in **all areas of your life.**

Therefore, know your Partner. Communicate with your Partner. Hold no other friendship or association to be greater than this Oneness you have with the God of the Universe. That which God gives is given unconditionally. There is no need to "earn" the right to use it or to keep it. There is no reason to wonder at your own abilities to manifest greatness, for the power, remember, comes from the Partner.

Bring your own teamwork into play. Note those areas of life and of the earth itself that need the greatness of Pure Truth which is there to answer every need. Now hold forth your hands to your Partner. Know they are grasped in the tender teamwork that unites you in an inviolate trust. You, master of greatness, are never unworthy. You are never unaware of this Partner. You are not an unimportant part of the association.

There must be this Partnership or there will be no personal touch of that which is the God of the Universe. The personal is through the Partnerships. The universal principles and laws which are God are the impersonal. Therefore, **you are important!** Apply Pure Truth to that which must be manifested and watch the God of the Universe go to work. The entering truth is what is God. You are that which personalizes it. God is that which powerfully produces the results.

Therefore, hold onto your understanding which we have explained to you. Otherwise, you will not feel the importance that is necessary for this partnership to work well. The way Jesus worked was with the positive assurance of the personal God, whom he called

"Father." Jesus understood God as the great power and truth that made manifestation of truth possible into the earth plane.

To repeat the same kind of manifestation that Jesus did so easily, you must work with the principles involved and team up with the law of God. We have discussed these in earlier books, but again, we will examine them here to enlighten you as to their supreme importance.

No eternal truth is without the compensating law that eternalizes it into the visible. Here is what we mean. The truth — that God brings purity into the earth — is held up against the law that insists that material objects in the earth plane must respond to truth. That means that the earth itself must enter into that law in order to survive as earth.

To wrest the understanding from these two statements, the one about the truth and the one about the law, you need to bring yourself into the earth to see it work toward purity. We did this in another book, "Masters of Greatness."[2] To accept this understanding is to know that the earth responds even now to that great truth concerning purity.

The writer asks if there is further proof of the law when people work diligently to purify the earth. People do work to hold back impurities and to use what is pure, but they, for the most part, act on their own. They work with the earth truth which has rules and great labor involved. The truth we speak of here calls forth the law exercising that truth into visible form. What we speak of is one thing, and what the writer asks about is another.

To enter into the partnership with authority, you must now burst forth with truth. The God Presence who is your Partner is the Source of that truth, and it is to Him that you must turn for the truth and the power to put it into earth form. Think on this partnership until you realize its worth, until you honor its existence as the only reality that matters. Then you will receive the understanding needed to produce truth into earth form.

We watch the process from this plane, but we can only help you with encouragement, not real help in attaining the truth into physical form. Therefore, you must study and perform on your own. When you have done this, you will be able to teach others. What a venture into wonderful creative truth! What an honest approach to the earth that is empowered by spirit to respond to the law of the universe that God has implanted!

Cautious optimism may now spread throughout the land with these words, but nothing will really happen until you open your mind with great tenderness to that which God IS. You will remain in absolute darkness on this matter until you embrace the true Light. Team up, you who would exercise yourselves as masters of greatness, team up to be what your mantle says you are — those who work with God to instate truth into the earth, into the people, into those situations of hopelessness because of earth truth.

Give yourselves fully to the open truth brought to you in this chapter through this writer who herself works to gain understanding. To offer you the opportunity to push beyond the inhibiting earth barriers, you must now perform in the marketplace of life. You must spend the truth that your Partner hands you with the abandon of a child who knows that there is much more to spend.

Give, masters of greatness, give again, because your supply is endless. Give until the bountiful truth spurts up through the soil into full view. Give until people praise the goodness, which is God, that restores their planet. Give, masters of greatness, to the point of finding no time for anything else! What is more important, after all, than the greatness of God being manifested in the earth?

Though the new polarity will still be needed, you can help to alleviate the situation by pouring truth upon the earth itself. Then you can open the eyes of people everywhere by holding the truth before their eyes expecting the law of the universe to translate that truth into a thousand tongues. Then people will rise in their understanding and cry aloud that God is indeed the host, the Perfect Truth that holds this planet in its place. They will be ready for the change, for the creative eternalization of the earth's restoration to purity.

But if the masters do not immediately go to work on this matter, people will proceed as they have always proceeded, using earth truth only, rising in their expectations to the level of their forefathers. They will not rise to the level of God understanding unless they receive Pure Truth. But the cause is not lost if the masters go to work even now. When the New Age comes, the masters will be accustomed to using Truth, and they will be able to execute what may seem at this reading to be too difficult.

Go to work now. Do not hesitate. Enter into the work of masters. Use the partnership to the fullest, for that is your responsibility. The one who uses the truth is YOU, not another person or other teamwork left to someone else. YOU are the responsible person. YOU will team up with your Partner Who will lead you in the greatest work you have ever done. Move into your position with authority, with the positive force of God Truth that waits to be used.

The writer hesitates now and then. The words enter her mind, but she rereads them to ascertain their meaning. She wants to work as we have stated, but now she tries to open her belief. To open her belief, she must exercise her responsibilities as a master of greatness.[3] She must see herself, not as an individual, but as the partner of that greatness which is God! She must hold herself as that energy which is guided and protected and given tender regard by the Teammate Who is now ready to work with her. This entity, this spirit / mind we call Truth-giver, is what is needed in the partnership if it is to become workable.

To reinstate truth into the planet earth, you must use

these Partnerships. Why form them only to wait until the New Age to use them? You must begin NOW to make use of them. You must begin NOW to open the resources of truth to the planet upon which you live.

The material in this chapter was so exciting that I shared it with a friend. This truth seeker wanted to know if ego alone can produce results with its own power. "Is there any feeling," this person asked, "of being on the right track when we send Truth into situations, the earth itself and into people?"

I asked for a response, and this is what came.

That which is asked here is not the Truth in action. When the ego sends forth its own power, it does not use God Truth at all. What can ego team up with? The ego enters with earth truth only. But earth truth is not the kind of Truth we speak of in this book, right? Negative truths would be a contradiction in terms, would they not?

The way we view the question is that when you who determine to work in Partnerships team up with every intention of proving the truth, then that truth will be proved. The one who asks has entered the more negative thought of ego into mind, but there is no real power with ego — except the power of earth-mind truth. Everyone can use earth-mind truth to accomplish many things, but eventually, that truth will peter out or turn into dead ends.

To prove the truth that God brings, each master must instate the truth with only the word, not with the force of personality, nor with a constant barrage of thoughts. The power to transform truth into the earth plane substance is not your responsibility. It is God's.

To begin your best efforts in manifesting truth, review the chapter Jesus gave you. Then review this one. Now is the time for you to begin the manifestation of truth — not in the time to come, not the day after tomorrow or the week after next. The time is coming to a close when you have the luxury of practicing with your truth.

Begin however you please, if you have not already

begun. Try to instate truth into whatever situation that now worries you with its lack of truth. Hold that situation or that person or that piece of real estate up to your Partner and say, "Here is my concern." Then gather into your mind the truth that applies to whatever you have chosen. When you place them side by side, the truth and the thought of a certain problem area, you are halfway through the manifestation process. Then turn to your Partner in confidence to do the rest — instate the truth into this thought you have presented.

During the writing of this chapter, a friend and I discussed the material I was receiving. Both of us were deeply convinced of its value. She spoke of one whom she cares about, one who was having an unsatisfying work experience. I suggested we forget the details and apply truth to the situation as this chapter has said. Therefore, we claimed the truth that each person may live a lifetime experience that reaches its maximum potential. We repeated this, affirmed it, knowing that this statement is certainly God Truth.

Then we applied it to the individual in this manner: Truth plus the mind / spirit of the individual plus God power equals the individual's expression of his potential.

After the conversation I wrote it all down in the notebook I use to record my communication with my Partner. I waited for a comment, and this is what came.

"My power holds all men, all creation. Trust My power. Leave the results to Me. Waken to truth bursting through. Waken to my son's center (the individual whom we named) blossoming forth. Watch it unfold! Open to My truth pushing through.

"Note how truth opens to realization, to greatness performing on strings of harmonic value. There opens a new life! The shell breaks open; the center unfolds; the being blossoms!

"Only truth can open the spirit. Only truth can send forth that which is born anew into a more teamed up mind. Climb upward to present truth; do not climb into the earth pattern.

"Now! Tenderly regard My wonderful handiwork!"

The communication ended, but I held a powerful light within me, a light more powerful than I have ever experienced.

The writer has shared in the personal, but those of you who now work must not share with others until you become strong enough to stand in the face of those who ridicule you, those who may turn away in embarrassment, those who even open their words against you. To share before you have personal strength is to weaken the value of your experimentation. The writer knows that by the time this book enters the marketplace, this situation will be resolved with perfection.

Work, meditate, then act! The time is near, masters of greatness, when you will be required to act with authority. Therefore, enter into the truth with great enthusiasm and with great understanding as you perfect your skills in manifesting truth in the earth plane.

[1] "Eternal Gold," 1988, from the **Trilogy of Truth**, Jean K. Foster; **TeamUp,** Warrensburg, Missouri.

[2] "Masters of Greatness," second book of **Truth for the New Age**, 1990; Jean K. Foster. **TeamUp,** Warrensburg, Missouri.

[3] Ibid.

Developing New Bodies for the New Age

6

New bodies reflect the perfection which God IS.

To enter the New Age with eternalizations of earth truth, you will team up with all that is adverse. However, to enter the New Age with the Truth of God shining forth through the spirit and into the body, is to create new and glorious bodies to live on the new and wonderful earth.

Your body has adapted itself to the earth plane that you now live in, has it not? The body eternalizes itself as perfect for the place where it lives. Therefore, perfection must be understood as that which is perfect for a certain place at a certain time! The entering truth helps each spirit to eternalize exactly what is needed in the place where he or she is. Bodies have changed throughout the centuries because of these eternalizations. Those who lived on the earth teamed up with truth that helped their bodies adjust to the earth itself which, in turn, was changing.

What we are trying to explain here is that the bodies of mankind will change significantly in the New Age to render them more useful to the spirit entities who enter the earth plane. Those who enter the body form will enter with eternalizations of how the body needs to perform. As that body grows, the spirit will make changes that will draw truth right into its form.

The New Age requires much more in the way of personal strength. Therefore, the body will enter into greater muscular ability because the spirit has recognized that need. The body will also need greater teamwork with its parts. This means that the various extensions such as hands, legs and feet will be better coordinated in order to facilitate man's mobility upon the new and changing earth. These new bodies will be glorious bodies that can inhale more air than most bodies do today. They will be more attuned to the vibrations that enter the earth plane through spirit.

People will grow new vegetables that have never been seen before, and they will grow all that is needed for these new bodies who no longer depend on meat for protein. Physical needs will be different. There will be less required in the way of minerals. Bodies will respond to vibrations to keep their good health or to repair what is broken or lacking in some way.

Also, those who work in the New Age will be better attuned to one another. They will enter into communication with their fellows without technical arts. The system they will use will depend on a finely attuned body that will receive messages sent to it. This new body will be totally incorruptible. That is, it will not enter into sickness or into drunkenness or into any kind of corruption. This body will team up with total goodness because it is that goodness in expression.

Gently bring yourself into this new time of conversion with anticipation of wonderful changes, masters of greatness, for the New Age will not be like the one you now experience. No! It will require more in the way of spirit and less in the way of physical needs. Your new body will be that of a builder who receives its orders through God-mind. This wonderful responsive body will team up with the universal greatness to create or to build whatever is required. We speak here not only of the body itself but of the environment.

It will not matter if you have a team of workers to assist you. That which you will be — that perfect body expression — will perform the tasks of many. Your body will vibrate to the tone of the Master Builder, the God of the Universe, and your body in its new strength will put plans into manifestation with ease and with little time involved.

What we paint here is a new way of life. What we bring before your eyes is the complete newness of the New Age. It will remain on this planet, yes, but it will restate all that the perfect alliance of man and God can bring into fruition. The body, masters of greatness, will be so changed within two generations that no books of medicine will be worthwhile. That which is new requires new thought, new understanding, new eternalizations.

The time of general turmoil approaches, and the earth bodies are little suited to what lies ahead. Therefore, begin now to eternalize your body undergoing many changes. One such change is that the new body must adjust to a gravity which will be less than the present gravity. That which is now considered as one hundred percent will be cut. The new gravity will be much less and will require more tone to your body. To accomplish this, you must have a sleek body form, one that will hold the organs gently in place. The gentle truth must open your body to new understanding on this matter.

To realize the benefits of less gravity, you only need to bring yourself into the experience of those who have ridden in space ships. They practiced without gravity, but you will have enough gravity that will enable you to maintain an upright posture. That you may adjust, we tell you to trim your bodies so that you will be firm and well toned muscularly.

To team up with the New Age, you must be ready to change. The entering truth of the Age will tell you many new truths about how to adjust your body. Then you will open your mind to accomplish that which will help you to live well.

I am the writer, not the author of this book. Sometimes the material impacts upon my mind to such an extent that I cannot continue to receive until I deal with what I have already written. Such was the case in this chapter when, at this point, the communication simply stopped because my mind leaped about picturing much less gravity and balanced distribution of my organs. Finally, the material continued.

At the time of earth change you will find very little gravity and sometimes none at all. Only the wind will hold you stable. Only the sanctuary of safe locations will help you to stay in place. When the earth stabilizes, it will have less gravity than it has ever known. We mention it now because there is time to work with this situation and become better suited to the less amount of gravity.

To maintain yourself in the New Age, your body must be able to conquer certain limitations. The New Age body must develop great lung power to inhale large amounts of air. The stomach, however, must grow smaller in order to ingest less food. The intestines will be better able to work with what the stomach sends to them, and there will be great food value in smaller amounts. The body will be more head centered and less stomach centered. The heads will shine forth with the light of the soul. With this light comes the purity of thought that translates itself into action, both within the body and within the planet.

Bright beings will begin to inhabit the earth, not the drab beings that inhabit it now. Those who originally were developed for the earth plane were inspired beings, but slowly they evolved into less bright bodies, less in tune with the universe. That which was given in the beginning was incorruptible. But slowly their bodies and minds dimmed, and their bodies lost their luster, lost their head centeredness, lost their vibratory tones.

Begin now, masters of greatness, to work with your bodies to bring them into that which we have described here. The bodies of the New Age will open to the perfection which is God. They will team up with their Partner to receive the open truth that will lead them into their potential. By working now to elevate your bodies, you will be able to attain that purity needed to enjoy whatever is pure.

By the time two generations have lived and then made way for another generation, the earth will reflect great handiwork. The potential of each individual will be reached, and great strides in true progress will be made. That which the earth now calls progress is only the earth truth that is accepted by all people. But what we speak of is the manifestation of great universal truth that is perfect for both the earth and for each person. The earth will be resplendent with bright beings who will be the new mankind and the true perfection.

The open truth that comes through this writer is probably not easy to assimilate. The writer remarked that when she first read it, she thought it wild and unbelievable. But when she went back over it, remembering that we have never brought lies or exaggeration to her, she teamed up with all that we have said. That may be the way it is with you, masters of greatness, as you try to project yourself into this New Age. The truth of it is, at first, overwhelming. But as you reflect, as you team up with your Partner to speak of your concerns, you enter into all that is presented. The open truth is remarkable in its wonder that raises your thinking each time it penetrates.

Now team up with your Partner to discuss each thought presented in this chapter. Reach out to know all there is to know about these events we mention, these facts that we project on the screen of the future. Then you will know how to work individually to be ready to hold these things in your heart that you may better serve mankind.

Thus ends this chapter, for there is much to consider here.

Life Styles in the New Age

7

Within two generations the planet will operate totally by God Truth.

Team up with God Truth, ye masters of greatness. Open your minds to the marvelous truth that will make the planet and the lives of people wonderful beyond compare. Gently we hand you this truth which opens to each master and to every open mind, for that matter, to make the New Age everything we have promised you.

In the New Age, you must enter into new truth. That's the summation of it. Today the earth venerates what is historically old as well as its progress — measured by earth wisdom. That which is old, however, will pass away as the sun enters the earth into its new orbit. That which will team up with the sun and the moon will become new in physical truth, and that which lives upon the earth will also be made new. Therefore, why cling to any of the old?

Museums offer people much to contemplate in the way of change. But yet they tend to think that the here and now is the epitome of what is perfect — or near perfect. But they enter into delusions, masters of greatness, for there is no misconception greater than the one that insists that the earth and its people have brought true progress upon the planet.

What has been wrought, in actuality, is the earth truth that insists there is no eternal truth, only so-called scientific answers. That which the earth names science is only the accumulation of earth truth — the poorest truth there is. Be prepared to open to what is new in the New Age, and have no regrets over truth that is lost. Better that it be lost than to be saved to corrupt the New Age!

Give time to eternalizations that prepare you to enter the New Age. Eternalize the new body as we told you in the previous chapter. Eternalize the new earth which is pure, fertile, ready for the creativity of God and man working as one. Then you will not regret what has passed away. The writer bemoans the expected loss of the great art galleries, the great repositories of earth knowledge and wisdom. But if these are saved, those who remain will undoubtedly worship at their shrines. Then the earth which will be so pure will have to endure the poor truth once again.

There is nothing of value that people need take with them into the New Age. There will be a time of peace, a time of good manifesting, a time of working with all that is pure and true to realize the truth in creative form upon the earth. Those of you who will go into the New Age must be ready to enter with authority, with the vision of true masters. Then people will turn to you as the teammate who has the answers, for indeed, you do!

Now turn your minds to the wonderful teamwork that will come about when you join others who prepare themselves to learn new ways of life. Those who turn their faces toward God Truth will resolutely not look back, for the truth will so astound them, even as it does you, that they will know new power, new happiness, new greatness.

Those who team up with you must learn to operate on their own. At the beginning, however, a cluster of devoted beings can help them to attain individual strength. Those who cluster will have visible support, but they will soon learn to hold fast to the invisible support. This invisible support is the gentle teamwork which we on this plane give to you on the earth plane. We will be here for you. We will help you to hold to your position as partners with that Teammate Who has the power, the strength, the wisdom and the understanding. We will help you by giving our counsel when asked, but always our mission is to unite you with God.

Now open your mind to new truth concerning the New Age. The Truth of God will be forthcoming steadily, and the teamwork will astound you in its power. Better teamwork will exist than you can now imagine, and the new earth will be that true paradise spoken of in the Bible. The new paradise is not the Garden of Eden (Genesis 2:10-15) that you have read about. The true paradise is that all pervasive truth is there to use, to see, to handle all of life's problems. People will laugh and sing freely. They will be open to everyone without fear of any other being.

There can be no crime, no punishment, no misunderstanding when people use God Truth. They will, even as we do in this plane, communicate by thought. Gone are the devious ways. Gone are the teams of people who plot against other teams. There will be no secrets. There will be some — not the masters — who do not like the sound of what we say. But those who have negative feelings have no notion of what free thought is like. They hide in their thoughts, give no hint of their own ideas, their own personalities. But in the New Age there will be no hidden thought! Therefore, there will be no means of hiding things, keeping secrets, holding back from true communication.

The new teamwork will be the paradise you enter into wholeheartedly. There will be tenderness that will be unbounded. There will be tender thoughts sent forth, tender gestures given, tender help extended. The new way of life will be paradise, for no one will feel lonely or left out of the group. Tender thoughts will so abound that each individual will be caught up in that understanding.

Problems that earth now has — poverty, homelessness, the displaced, people who want economic power — will not exist. People will work to give good to all. Why hoard? What is there to gain? Thoughts of bringing the good of life to those who may still be trying to manifest it will be the foremost business of the New Age. No one will be left to flounder about in ignorance in view of the bountiful success others have in manifesting.

The entering truth in the New Age will team up with people everywhere, not people who live in one part or another part of the planet, as if they have a corner on truth. The eventual way of the earth will find people scattered all over the planet. People who were once in one place will be in another, and there will be such a mixture of peoples that the only hope is to communicate with thought. The languages will be a hindrance, and therefore, people will rise in their understanding as you masters lead them to communicate in thought.

There will be some who will try, at first, to organize groups of people according to old ways. They will reach out with persuasive words and gather quite a group together. This kind of authority, however, being based on the old earth truth, will not hold any promise for the new earth and the new mankind. There will be no interest in this kind of production because it simply will not work. Therefore, people will be more inclined to turn to that new way of teaming up to accomplish whatever it is they wish to accomplish.

The family unit will not be the same. The writer has been sending us signals asking about the family, but we have ignored her because this part will be hard for her to understand. The New Age will not promote families in the way the present society promotes families. The reason for this change is that families have instigated much in the way of terrible rivalries and bad emotional ties. Generations of families hold thoughts of vengeance against other families. The people of the earth, in order to experience God Truth, must rid themselves of these ideas of family pride, family loyalty and the like.

The writer hears all this sorrowfully, for she thinks families are the mainstay of the life in the world as she sees it. But yet she recognizes the truth of what we say. The family unit is too small, too ingrown, too much centered on itself to perpetuate much good. Therefore, the New Age will have peoples clustering together who want to bring truth upon the earth. They will recognize their oneness with God, their teamwork with that wonderful greatness that is universal truth.

The writer persists. "Where is the position of the child in all this?" she wonders. We comment on the truth of this question in order not to hide anything from the masters of greatness. We know what we explain here will be hard to understand due to your involvement with the way things are in the present age. There will be children in the clusters, but they will not be the total responsibility of one or more individuals. Children will not come into the world in exactly the same manner as those who have previously populated the earth. No, the child will be the product of earnest teamwork of those who want to give space to an entering spirit. They want the spirit to contribute to the overall good of their cluster, but mainly they will want it to contribute to the overall good of the planet and mankind.

The writer is appalled! Yet we must present the picture with accuracy. The teamwork you call sex in the earth plane is only the outward expression of entering tenderness, if that tenderness wants to express. But it is also the expression of mankind's desire for closeness to another person. The new tenderness will be teamed up with each person to the point where no expression of sex is needed to temporarily give the illusion of tenderness. Therefore, that kind of sex will disappear. There will be no accidental babies entering the earth plane. They will be planned.

Those who want to mother the children will be given

that responsibility. Those who have used the teamwork to create well-toned bodies will be sought to bring forth the child body. Therefore, the creating of children will be a responsibility, not a thing that happens whether or not mankind wants it. Those who bear the children may take care of them, or they may not. There will be those who nurture well, and they may be given that responsibility. The main thing is to give nurturing and care on a continuous basis. The welfare of the child is put above the individual tenderness. Family relationships will not matter, for people will welcome this better way.

The thought is hard to express, for unless you have experienced that total tenderness which is God, you will not be able to understand this great difference in the style of life. By the time two generations have passed through the New Age, new truth will be well instated, and the old useless earth truth will have passed away. Those who live the abundant life will receive the tenderness of God that will fully satisfy, and their bodies will become centered in the upper parts, not the lower parts. That is why sex — just as sex — will disappear. This function will be attached to the higher level of mankind who uses sex for the purpose it is intended — to create more bodies for incoming spirits.

We do not expect you to understand it all right now. We cannot expect you to truly embrace the New Age in totality. But if we would keep some things from you now, we would not be adequately preparing you to meet the future.

The writer wonders about individual relationships, the love one man and one woman may find together, for example. This teamwork will become much different than it is in the old way of life. The teamwork will be centered in God Truth, God satisfactions, God understanding. Therefore, do not try now to perfectly understand the difference. Only know that when the old passes away, the new will bring totally different expectations, totally different methods, totally different relationships.

The next chapter will talk about relationships, masters of greatness, and perhaps then you will gather the insight you need to project the new life style. Team up with us as we bring you this chapter to know that we never bring you what is untrue or what is unnecessary. We team up with you to bring the truth that will set the tone you must identify with if you are to enjoy the New Age. The transition is the hard part, but it is to you that the responsibility is given to make it safely through the time of turmoil into a stable environment. And it is to you the "keys" are given to understand why things are different.

When you tell people that it was written that all this would happen, they will believe you. When you tell them how they can cooperate with the way things are, they will want to do whatever you say to them. Whenever you project the life to come, they will embrace the projections. This way people will know there is planning and good sense in all that happens. They will trust that power behind the change to fulfill the promises of the New Age.

Masters Learn Their Roles as Leaders

8

Those who are to lead others will learn how to calm the turmoil and how to work in the face of opposition.

The truth that you receive through the open channel will bring you everything you need in the way of proper understanding. This Truth of God-mind is centered in the teamwork of you, the God of the Universe and the Brotherhood. To use this truth effectively, those who enter the New Age must be taught the procedure for bringing whatever they want and need into the earth plane.

People will begin by disbelief, masters of greatness, for they may never have had experience with God Truth. They may ridicule that which you say. They may try to blame you for their own poor condition. This basic need many people have to blame others for their own problems must be met with firmness on your part.

Team up with this Brotherhood to receive advice and counsel if you meet this kind of resistance. They — those who bury their good — will only be convinced by your own work with truth. Therefore, do not hesitate to produce it. They will be eternalizing hopelessness, and they will be eternalizing the search for supplies buried beneath the earth. But you will enter into no turmoil, no earth-mind organization that may be underway. You will calmly become one with the appropriate truth needed to produce, and then, with your Partner, you will be open to great understanding that will fulfill your purpose.

They — the earth organizers — will stand amazed. They will turn and twist about finding explanations to satisfy themselves and others. Enter into no dialog with them save the invitation to eat, or to share shelter, perhaps. They — these unnamed ones — will give you your due, though grudgingly. They will gently hold your being before them with new thoughts, and perhaps they will then be ready to learn for themselves. But if not, ignore their words and go your way.

Those who join you in the cluster of beings who turn to new truth must hold to that purpose. Their survival depends on their understanding of what is said here. Those who make the cluster uneasy with their assaults on the truth must leave. There is no way we can prepare you for this time except to tell you of it. These times will require action, and those who oppose you will team up with ideas which will lead to beggarly conclusions. Therefore, they will condemn their own truth by inadequate results.

Masters must turn always to their Partners. They must dialog with those of us here who can help in this difficult time when the earth teams up with a new point of polarity. Be thoroughly centered. Be resistant to your own being who may wish for the old way of life. You must resolutely point the way to the new life, and therefore, you must be centered.

Be true to your mantle, master of greatness. Team up with all that you know and understand. Then begin to teach others bit by bit while you provide for their needs. There will be some who fairly leap to be your students. There will be a nucleus group who will surround you and will protect you from those who would hurt you. Yes, there will be some who, because they are impotent in those times, will want to hurt you.

That mind set will exist until they either change or until they bring their souls to this plane.

Changing to the Truth of God will take time because many who survive will have no notion of how gentle beings can bring forth wonderful truth to the earth. They will not even recognize that which is good because they will be fixed upon the past. To them the eternalization should be one of power that is centered in the few with the rest opening themselves to the leadership of that few. To resist this kind of potential chaos, all you do is to walk away. There will be no force except that of brute strength applied by hands that will try but which will not be able to hold you.

The writer insists on knowing why the hands cannot hold you. The new teamwork of earth, sun and moon will present less gravity, and there will be those who will not understand how to use it. They who want to hurt you will reach out to bodily manhandle you, but you will simply leap through the crowd because you will work with the forces that have entered the earth. Those who want to hurt you, remember, are not working with the New Age. They work against whatever is new.

The new gravity will team up with everyone slowly, and at first there will be little control. Then as you teach them control — by thought — you will gather the beings that want all truth at their command. They will see that there is truly only one way to survive, and they will, at last, turn to you. But as we said, there will be those who surround you and protect you. They will be volunteers who will enter the earth plane with their bodies to help you with your work if the need is there. Now that you understand that the Brotherhood is able to do whatever is needed to help you, know that your task is simply to keep on with your work. You will receive help with everything that worries you. Team up with what we say here!

Team up now to go further with this truth that you will teach. The initial time will be the hardest — the time when the earth begins to stabilize — because the earth will not team up with what people think they know, and they will be afraid they will starve or that the elements will overcome them. They will turn to one another with endless questions. But you will not take leadership in the way described above by those who force that leadership upon others. The leadership we speak of is that which naturally comes about when a master of greatness tenderly approaches the problems and then quietly brings forth the proof of leadership — truth that manifests as the satisfactory solution.

Be entirely calm. Be entirely certain of your partnership. Team up with the Brotherhood. The resources you call forth will open the endless supply which people need. The resources you depend upon will give whatever is needed to each person, whether or not that person believes that truth can manifest.

Now listen to what we say about teaching those students who proclaim their readiness to learn. They will be ready because they feel desperate, but they might not heed what you say. Therefore, begin by helping them become centered and calm within. Then they will be able to hear what you say and to accept it. Centering is absolutely needed or the teaching is in vain. They will want to know the Source of their good. Then they will want to know what magic words to say. They will also want to have you there with them to do the manifestation. There will be no way to answer so many requests.

There will be too many demands upon you, masters of greatness, to answer them all. Therefore, we recommend that the way to put the situation into perspective is to begin with the elemental things of life — those things that will be required to live. With this in mind, you will immediately sort out those requests that need your attention and those that do not. Team up with all requests that have to do with prolonging life itself — nothing more. Then hold classes when you can. By working with those who have specific life needs, you have automatic classes. Those people will give you their full attention, their immediate and continuous concentration, because what they want is important to life.

By using this method, you will have those who finally open their minds to the Truth of God. These people will be your advanced class who will then manifest for themselves. You will teach them how to open the minds of others. Then, as they work to manifest for themselves, they will take on another person who is quite dependent upon you, thus relieving you of one responsibility. This way the dependent one learns the rudimentary truth of the New Age, the truth that will impose greatness into the earth plane, the truth that will enter the earth with the majesty of God Who understands that good must be expressed when it is called forth.

At this point you will have many others working with truth, opening to their own truth, and they will be making great advances. They may grow egotistical along the way, and when they do, remind them that manifestation only takes place when people use the qualities of God — generosity, tenderness, thoughtful understanding, teaming up with others to bring good into the earth plane. Never chastise them, masters of greatness, or they will grow to hate that which is said to them. They will neglect their study and fall into disrepair. That is, they will enter into untruth and their bodies will fail, and their truth will be ineffective in the earth plane.

Do as God does — hold no condemnation toward others. They may take hold of truth and grow mightily, but then they will fall back. Have you not the same problem with yourself? The New Age requires much of masters because it is they who must lead the others. Therefore, ready yourself by holding the truth to your bosom, and release all thoughts of anger, dislike, hate. No one can soar with God who burns with poor emotions that reflect earth truth.

Now turn to what is needed within yourself to hold to the truth. That which you need is reassurance that you do what God wants you to do. The Brothers stand ready to reassure you or to advise you or to counsel with you. Their tenderness is yours. Their affection is yours. But you may want the affection, the friendship of human beings. We present this idea to you because we see it now in those who team up with truth. Therefore, we give you this formula to apply to your life experience to find those who can be true friends.

To find those who can join you in true affection, open your mind to the need you have for that person, male or female, with whom you can share your life. We do not speak of getting married. No, you will not marry. But the point is that you want to share your spiritual journey — to lead your cluster into new life upon the planet. This person will share your gentle truth, be open to receive what you have to give, will share with you the concerns that he, or she, may have. That is the true friend, right?

The thought has gone forth. The mind is open and ready. The Partner wants this person to appear in your life. Give yourself to the power of your Partner and become still. The eternalization will be given you of the kind of being you seek. Heed the details and fix them into your mind. Then you will know that this person will be drawn to you to become your true friend. That which has been brought together in this way will bring you much peace.

To enter the New Age with success, you must be ready, masters of greatness. To attain this readiness, offer your present truth to the earth plane with the vigor that will be required in the New Age. When you have become truly proficient in this better understanding, you will stand ready for any emergency. Team up with those who address you now, those who understand the earth plane as well as the spirit self. Those who live in earth bodies enter into the New Age with misgivings, with misunderstandings. They have no recognition of the God who must bring purity into the earth, who must call forth that which is good to rise to the surface where it will be wholeness personified.

People will react by teaming up with whatever they have within them.

There will be some who eternalize the end of the world, and they will probably die. There will be some who think the earth is undergoing an atomic fissure, and they will seek shelter and try to survive somehow. There will be some who think God is sending punishment, and they will submit without struggle. These, too, will probably die. But there will be many who struggle to survive because it is their nature to do so. They will be your group.

They will stand amazed that they are whole, or nearly whole. Those who team up because they are there together will want some reassurance, some kind of optimistic act. This is where you step forth with whatever is most needed. This is the time to pour truth upon the earth where it will immediately blossom. Why will it work so quickly? Because the new purity is unresistant to truth! Had you thought of this before? Had you realized why it is that you will accomplish with ease what now is most difficult?

The seeming miracle is that the truth will enter with alacrity because there will be absolutely no resistance. The writer recalls the time when Jesus' mother asked him to change the water into wine. Did the earth, she wonders, team up with good then? Was the earth itself pure?

Jesus could manifest truth easily because there was no resistance; that is right. Transforming the water into wine was easy for him because his mother sweetly teamed up with the truth which Jesus used. Also, Jesus held his truth so lightly in his mind that he could easily make whatever he wished if it were for good. The earth was not impure! There was much purity. But the people had become corrupt, unable to turn to the reality of God or the reality of themselves — spirit.

To act with the truth you have, non-resistance is needed (in order) to attain the goals perfectly. That does not mean that each person in the cluster need approve, nor does it mean you must take a vote! No!

The purity is within you, within the earth itself, and those who cluster about have no reason to object when you are serving their needs. Therefore the truth will fairly leap out to perform its task.

Understand your truth as the wisdom of the ages, wisdom that God placed within the earth in its beginnings. This truth will be easy to use, for it was created by God for the earth plane, and it was meant for the creative operation of earth and life.

Now heed this understanding: No person can do his job if he is not prepared! Therefore, work now, masters, to become proficient in truth that is put to work in the earth plane. That which goes into earth is now under the protection of the Brotherhood who work with you to announce the coming Age. Team up to wrest your truth NOW into the earth. Enter it; work with it; throw caution to the wind! That which God intends must be put to work. Therefore, practice the generosity that God IS, and bring truth into service.

The Wholeness Concept Never Fails

9

Those who will work with the healing arts must embrace the larger concept of God wholeness.

Team up with this chapter to understand the totality of the healing arts as practiced by God Truth. That which now opens to you is not eternalized in the earth plane today, but it must be eternalized in the earth plane in the New Age. Why? Because only the Truth of God will work in this new and uncorrupted earth.

To recognize the effects of God Truth, you must understand that the New Age opens itself to pure spirit, to pure thought projection, to a better understanding of what this earth truly is and what it means in relationship to mankind. Vested interests — like the medical professions — will no doubt team up with the truth they have already learned about the body. But they must recognize that mankind will be developing bodies that are much different than the present body. Therefore, concepts of medicine must change.

Those who now practice medicine must, in one way or another, team up with God Truth to learn how to help people in the age to come. They must open themselves fully to the Partner who will instruct them anew in the healing arts. They may, if they wish, take on this concern of healing and repairing, tenderly helping those whose bodies have become inoperable. If they want to stay with the healing arts, however, they must embrace the larger concept of God wholeness.

Here is how wholeness will operate in the earth plane after the New Age has begun. At first the human body will be beset with changes. But because of the new purity in the earth, people will receive whatever benefits that purity has to give — which will be substantial. Those whose bodies have templed with negative vibrations will learn how to reach out for positive vibrations.

These positive vibrations are the energy and the tone of the earth itself — that which is truly of God, that which is truly spirit. When people have accepted this truth, they will use it as they would use any truth. This is the understanding which you must pass on to those in the New Age, masters of greatness. In the New Age when you meet a person who has worked in healing arts, one who may be discouraged because he or she has no medicine or technical helps doctors and nurses are used to, tell that person the following story.

Say that there was once a wonderful hospital in the earth plane, one that hired only people who had learned that God IS that wholeness that we all want to be. These doctors, nurses, medical technicians — everyone there — turned first to that God concept of wholeness. They also used earth truth. But now — in the New Age — the hospital has fallen and the earth is not as it was. Therefore, those who once manned the huge hospital now must go forth without that facility. But what do they have left? The greatest concept that ever was — the God concept of wholeness!

These people took the concept and worked with it night and day. Those who came for help found help. Those who wanted healing found healing. Those who previously entered into the idea of disease found themselves free of any symptoms. No, this is not a miracle story, masters of greatness. This story is told here so you may tell it to those who think all is lost. That which is truly effective, that which people truly need is not lost at all. There it is — within your mind / soul where you can use it over and over.

Take this concept within your being and let it grow there. Team up with this concept until it abides within your being like money resides within the bank. There will be interest in the form of wellness of your own body. Ideas of goodness will be expressed right within a body that responds to the concept. Therefore, work now with this concept, place it within your own being and let it begin its greatness.

The writer wishes she knew more about medicine or healing so she could ask questions such as doctors might ask. Go with us now to a hospital. Within this earth hospital are many machines that do each task with perfection. When the machine has done whatever it can do, then the doctor enters. Though machines do wonderful diagnostic tasks, the doctor must prescribe the procedure to be used to effect cures. Those who are ill want to have doctors, not machines, team up with their needs. They want that which is teamed up with spirit. They want the partnership of one who enacts the healing arts.

In the New Age one does not have to be a doctor to pass along the wholeness concept, but at first many people will be more comfortable with those who had been doctors. Therefore, it is to them that we now address this story that they may give their attention to it. Then they will reach out in wisdom to learn this method. Masters of greatness who have personnel from hospitals may enroll them in wholeness learning to teach them what is closest to their hearts and their interest. They will give you their attention, masters, when they see that what you tell them works.

Here is how you teach them. There will be someone in your midst who has become hurt or otherwise has physical suffering. Take this individual into the "hospital" arena where the medical people will stand with you. To the patient you will say, "The earth we stand on has purified to such an extent that we breathe purity into our bodies where it effects all kinds of healing. Team up with this question: What do I want to happen to my body? Think carefully. Team up with those of us standing here and tell us what you want to happen."

There may be some hesitation because this person is used to waiting for the doctor to say what is possible and what is not. Insist, however, that the patient respond to the question. If the leg is apparently broken and useless, the mere stating of this fact will not be enough. What does the person want the leg to do? Perhaps the person will then begin to see what must be done and answer like this: "I want my leg to be straight. I want the bones to knit, to become whole, to allow me to stand upright and to work. I want this leg to be perfect."

What a wonderful statement! And you must tell the person so. "What a clear and good statement," you think toward the patient. Enter this clear thought into your mind, and hold it there while others standing here also think how perfect this leg can be. If there are any who shake their heads, turn them out of the operating arena. Then waiting there with strong eternalizations, know that the Partner works with power to enter into the visible exactly what the patient eternalized.

Then those who stand there with you will understand the way it must be. The patient is the key here. Next is the eternalization of what the patient wants expressed. You act only as the guide, masters of greatness, the guide for the patient to express healing. There may be some who understand what you have done, and they will open themselves to this work also. But there may be others who see it all as magic, and they will always turn to you or to others who stand by. Those who open themselves fully to what you have done may not truly understand what has happened. They will do as you have done, but if they only mimic you instead of understanding the truth of wholeness, they will not team up with that healing and wholeness that people need.

The use of thought in the New Age is comparable to using thought in this next plane of life. There will be a great relationship between the two planes, even as there existed in the beginning of human life upon the earth.

Eternalizations will abound when it is understood, masters of greatness, and there will be some who go wild with the power! But they will fail to continue, and they will even become impotent because they will fail the test of God Truth. They will fail to use it with the understanding of who and what God IS — total perfection, total goodness, total generosity, the perfect alliance with all that is Godlike. When they fail, they will say they have lost their power, or they may say that God has capriciously taken the power away. But these reasons will be erroneous.

The reason many will fail to continue with greatness is that they enter into truth selfishly. There will be some who eternalize the way their bodies might be if they would have new faces or new muscles or any new parts. They may turn away from helping others and instead, they may help only themselves to new beauty, new charismatic endeavors that will attract others to themselves. But do not worry about these, masters of greatness, for they will consume themselves by their own volume of personal requests that will only enhance the individual. They will lose their power because they do not understand it, not because God is angry.

The open truth here is that the wholeness concept, when applied in like manner with God as the mentor, will never fail to do that which it is given to do. Team up with this understanding! Those who invoke the power of their Partners and eternalize the wholeness concept for the person or the condition or the earth or the animal will team up with understanding even as the earth teams up with the sun and the moon. Those who understand the purity of the New Age must know that to ally themselves with truth is to guarantee manifestation.

The writer wonders at this point how we can practice with this concept now — before the New Age. We team up with you who invoke this concept to help you apply it in the here and now. The spirit helpers will know how to lift truth into the powerful God concept that will enable a person, condition or the earth itself to become whole.

The writer wishes more on this matter because she knows of many individuals who need that concept applied to their bodies, their spirits, their entire lives. Those whom you want to lift up into the God concept of wholeness must already have certain expectations — healing or a hopeful attitude, perhaps, or even a thought of becoming whole.

You may then apply wholeness as a concept to their expectations! If their expectations are weak, wholeness will attack the mind set to try to open it to the wisdom of the truth itself. If the person has expectations of healing, then the wholeness concept may limit itself to just that healing — not turning over the entire being, or self, into God Truth. Use the wholeness concept whenever you wish, masters, but realize that you only send forth what is the potential, not the actual happening. The concept plus the expectation plus the power of God at work in the concept will produce whatever is possible, subject only to the imposed limitations of the individual in question.

Team up with whatever truth you want to apply to conditions and to people, but realize that though you are firm in your understanding, and God is true to the promise of power working that truth into manifestation, the individual who has free will can block those powerful aspects of truth.

Put your mind to work here. Put your mind into the wonder of the Partner who has the partnership well in Mind. Then go to work. Team up with the needs and the truth wherever you can. Then watch the Partner go to work. Within each individual is that source of wisdom, the God self, who wants to team up with truth. Therefore, address that God self. Tenderly approach that self, and promise the partnership's power in bringing truth to bear upon the problem.

Now practice, masters of greatness, and you will see results. Then know that when the New Age comes, you will work more easily because the earth will be pure and will reach forth for God Truth. Wholeness will more easily be made known. Now it may be hidden from many eyes, but those of you who make use of the concept will see the results and will rejoice.

Be certain that you have the wholeness concept well in mind. Review it now to help your mind strengthen its understanding. Remember, wholeness results when the individual holds a wide view of God — so wide that there is no encompassing that Being or that principle or law. Therefore, keep your entity in tune with the infinite which is God. Then know that this concept is the principle with which you work to attack problems that are caused by inferior truth. Open, of course, to the power of God which will push this concept right into whatever situation or person you want reached.

The concept of wholeness is the principle, and the truth is that wholeness must appear in all life, in people, in plants, and in the earth itself. Why? Because they are all that which is God — they are that which is one with God. Therefore, there is no question of the rightness of wholeness, is there? That which is not whole must respond to wholeness because it is of God. The power will manifest when the concept or truth is laid onto the situation or person. The power will release this wholeness into that which turns to the God concept of wholeness.

If a person does not want wholeness, you will be working in vain. But yet the person may change, may open himself to the open channel and God-mind truth. By now you have had experience with this work, no doubt. Team up with all truth and their concepts. The time to use them is now, but when the New Age arrives, they will be your library of eternalizations that will open truth to the earth plane.

I interrupted the flow to ask questions.

"How can I help another person who is open to the wholeness concept, but who does not perfectly understand it?" was my first question.

The response was immediate. "That which is given, is given whether or not the other person understands it. The one who must understand it, however, is you, a master of greatness. To give it, you must have it teamed up within you. Therefore, the responsibility is yours to have this concept within your mind, Truth-giver! Then when you suggest this concept to others, you can explain what it is and how it works in a person's life."

I asked another question. "Recently I spoke of wholeness to two people and I explained what it is. But I did not know exactly how to send this concept to them with the power of God. What, if anything, is the individual who receives the wholeness principle supposed to do to be whole?"

"There is nothing anyone DOES," the Brotherhood replied. "The incoming wholeness is powered by the Partner, the God of the Universe whose concept it is. Therefore, what you do when talking to another person is to give the individual the wholeness concept which teams up with the need or the situation by itself. It — the wholeness — does this because it must enact itself somewhere when pulled forth in the way you mention. The power that your Partner applies is the natural act, not one you must remind Him of! The wholeness concept, plus the need or situation you focus it on, plus the power of the Partner produce wholeness in that object, that person or that animal you team up with."

"And that's it?" I asked. "Simply enter the truth to the situation and watch God power perform?"

"Be assured that truth needs your entire attention, however," came the reply. "Team up with wholeness, with the Source of all good, with the God of the Universe whom you cannot even imagine in all the greatness possible. If you use truth as a sometime thing, you are not serious about truth! What we speak of here is the totality of truth. Wholeness is one of these. However, it is very important to you as the

New Age begins because people will be suffering from disabilities due to the turbulence. They will require wholeness to go forward.

"What bothers you, Truth-giver? Is it that you wish to see it working now? How many times have you pushed this concept into those who could use it?"

"To be honest," I replied, "only four or five times since the Brotherhood explained it to me. Before that I appealed to God for healing."

"When you have entered the truth concept of wholeness thirty or forty times," the Brotherhood admonished me, "you may begin to understand and not tiptoe about afraid to act with power!"

As usual, the counselor/teacher spoke directly to my inner self. Would I ever learn enough? Could I ever enact the role of master?

"Do not berate yourself. Hold onto each new meaning you gather in order to learn. Team up now with wholeness, not just for the few whom you know but for the many who will reach your attention. Then enter wholeness on behalf of those who cannot enter it for themselves because they are ignorant of the concept or they are too much into other church truth that has certain requirements set forth. Team up with wholeness and put it to work.

"Be the master of greatness who pours truth out upon the ground in order to improve that ground. Do not count the defeats, but pay attention to the successes. There may be some defeats in the sense that nothing happens. But who knows why nothing happens? Turn to the successes to learn why they succeed. That way you will learn much."

The Brotherhood returns to the reader.

This chapter is to help you to stretch beyond your present use of truth and become one who cannot stop using it. To be a true master, practice and practice. Then success will team up with you and you will learn why.

Tending the Pure Truth

10

The only way to keep truth within the planet is to guard it night and day.

New truth which will team up with all the eternalizations that people make in the New Age will remain pure if those who use it guard it night and day. That which is the gold of the universe must not be wasted nor poured into unwholesome vessels.

New Age truth is not different from truth now, masters of greatness. You who have become masters have studied the truth, worked with it, entered into our full teamwork. But in the New Age, haste will mean that many will be using truth without realizing its value or understanding fully what they do. Therefore, we send this warning to those of you who may underestimate the need for watchfulness over the Pure Truth.

No God Truth in and of itself can be bad. Nor can any use of truth be bad because the Pure Truth only manifests when used by those who open to all that God IS. Yet there are ways to corrupt the truth. When people learn to use it and bring forth their needs, they will try to reach into that truth for power. We bring you this message because we have seen this corruption before. The corruption itself is not within the truth, masters. The corruption occurs when people twist the truth and call it their own invention.

There will be some who insist that God Truth is just a matter of the earth being ready for pure thought. Those who embrace this kind of thinking have no realization of what they do. They are, in effect, creating a whole body of earth truth once again. The Pure Truth is spirit; it is power; it is naturally good. To twist Pure Truth to make it a half truth or an inaccurate statement of belief is the danger we speak of.

Bring new openness to what we say because it is not easy to understand. The Pure Truth is not set out before you or anyone because you deserve it, remember. The Pure Truth IS. It performs because it IS what it IS, not because of anything you do to cause it to perform. Some people, and there will be some, will team up with the idea that anyone may make full use of Pure Truth. They will begin to play with the powerful eternalization that enters the truth into the planet.

They will think, "What can be wrong with this?" Or, "Why can't I have a little fun?" They may begin to move the truth here and there to form certain things that are for their pleasure. They will deny that they work for their own pleasure and claim that they work for everyone. But when they begin to bring forth those things that people do not want or need, but things that would merely give momentary pleasure, perhaps, then you masters know it is time to enter the situation.

Remind people of the gifts that are theirs when they use them with eternalizations that reflect the wisdom and nature of God. Then hold them responsible for the things they do. "Truth," you will tell them, "enters you now, but the truth you create is not God Truth. It is your truth, that which becomes earth truth. Therefore, what you do is not to be taken lightly because your own endeavors show that you use, not God Truth, not Pure Truth, but a truth that you yourself create. You, the individual being who has a plan to work through, must undo the damage you have centered within the planet. Remove it."

These people may hear you or they may not. If not, send the open channel that will team up with each individual and hold that person firmly in God-mind. Be assured that there is no pain here, no punishment, no outward problems. Put your trust in our Brotherhood that we may be helpful in removing the speck from our brother's eye that he may see clearly when it comes to using truth.

Never do we harm anyone's body. We will only help the spirit to center, even as we help your spirits to center, until the Pure Truth once again flows through.

Pure Truth will be your means of pulling creative energy into the planet to enter greatness once again. But if even one individual begins to misuse this truth, earth mind will take on importance and will begin to influence those who eternalize amiss. Remember, earth-mind truth today has much to commend it because people have brought much energy into it, but yet it is not the wholesome truth that God has in store.

If earth-mind truth takes hold, it will encourage people to boast, and it will lead them to desire power over others. It will lead to competition which misused Pure Truth to the point that the open channel will close and become forgotten. There must be vigilance, masters, vigilance and great concern over the protection of that which is Pure Truth.

Even now you must guard your own truth. Isn't that right? Even now you must hold up your truth to the Light that keeps it pure and bright. Even now you must go into your private temple to work through those things that want to sever Pure Truth and bring in some outcast version of it.

Team up with us to realize that only vigilance can keep truth pure. Only your watchfulness can keep it open to God and closed to corruption. Those who eternalize amiss will begin the corruption. Those who team up with selfish desire will turn God Truth into each man's pleasure. Those who open themselves to corrupt thought team up to realize their own fruits — destruction. But they leave behind them that body of earth truth that can corrupt others.

To get rid of such truth once the perpetuators have

left the scene, team up with your Partner to undo the corruption. Teaming up with those who know how to rid the earth of corruption will enable the goodness of God to prevail once again without the turmoil caused by bestial earth truth.

The writer wonders why people did not watch over their truth the last time the earth moved on its axis in response to a different polarity. We have tried to explain this occurrence in other books she has written. However, perhaps we should team up with her now to give an explanation once again.

That which was once pure in the planet was given to those offshoots of God to produce all that they thought good. They entered into the earth with responsibilities, but some began to play with creative energy, and eventually this energy dissipated from the planet. They entered into animal forms because it was so easy to do. They and the animals romped and played, but because those offshoots of God became more and more earth centered, they lost their ability to remove themselves except by bringing the animal to physical destruction.

These acts and others brought people into disrepair, and they even began hateful practices which brought pain upon them. These wondrous spirits who were once so free and lovely became lost in a maze of earth truth with which they themselves bombarded the earth. Freedom is the key to great happiness, but it may also be the key to great destruction. That is why watchfulness must be the keynote of the New Age.

I stopped the transmission to review. What happens to the planet when people become immersed in earth truth? What are the changes?

Those who began with great wisdom will remain wise. Those who turn to foolishness will team up with whatever seems interesting, not what is good or wise. But if the foolish ones are allowed to play with truth, experiment with their selfishness, dishonor the Pure Truth with their entities primed and ready to become beings of inferior truth, the planet will become teamed up with a body of unworthy beliefs. People will become caught between earth truth and Pure Truth. Polarity of opinions will emerge, of course, but those who stir the earth with their half truths will make the beings upon that earth separate into individual entities who again seek what is theirs by right — God-mind Pure Truth.

There will be confusion instead of true goals expressed. There will be those who try to take over because people know not what to do, which way to turn. Then the earth will indeed reenter the times that caused it to regain its purity, and again people will travel the worn road, anxious and uneasy. Yes, the fruits of entry into earth truth are anxiety and uneasiness.

But now you are forewarned, masters of greatness! Now you know what can happen if you turn your eyes from the center or allow others to do so. Enter into no close associations with those who try to corrupt your own thinking. Those you can count on are here in the Brotherhood of God. They will help people keep their center bright and pure, and if those who want to change things open others to their way of thinking, they must indeed pay the price. The price is, of course, teaming up with them to open them to this Brotherhood. There will be no inquisition, no opinions that will attack them or give them hard lessons. No! The Brotherhood will merely besiege those who turn to error thoughts and keep turning their minds toward God-mind Truth. Then they will reemerge as new creations to recant their earth-mind ways and to go forward with greater zeal than anyone!

The writer stands amazed at what we say here. To wrest earth truth from their minds seems impossible to her, but we know that when the new purity occurs, people's minds will be opened to us and we can make ourselves heard. To stand back and only shake our heads when God Truth is corrupted is not to take our responsibility, is it? Then remember what we say here.

That which will pull the wrong thinking back into right thinking is the mind to mind work we will undertake.

Nothing of error thinking must get into the new earth, masters. The Pure Truth is the truth to put into motion, into the earth substance which will prove itself in the perfection and the greatness that manifests. We who stand ready to help know our part. We will help as you call upon us. The other part is your responsibility — to call upon us to help. Remember, we only act when you call. We never force ourselves upon your thinking, upon your mind, upon your desire to think through to a decision.

Your right to private thoughts is there, masters, but understand that your thoughts may be picked up by others in the earth plane. The way to reserve space for yourself is to hold a secret rendezvous within your private temple where you enclose it with sound proofing material. Then use this space to think on various subjects until you are ready to be open.

Openness is good because once you emerge from the private temple, you can easily communicate with others. But you must learn to control your thoughts. Those racing thoughts that present your mind as one who knows no discipline will be turned off by others. "This person chatters constantly," they will say of you if your thoughts race uncontrolled. "Wisdom is there, but so is foolishness," others will remark. Therefore, learn control; learn to concentrate, to form thoughts that are considered and well advised.

Hold firmly to truth. Concentrate on truth. Hold it to the light of the Partner who is the Source of all. Team up with the Brotherhood to listen, not to talk aimlessly. Put the matter of soul growth — yours — as the principle business of each day, masters. Then you will stay centered.

Each entering truth will form itself to your understanding; therefore, do not fear that there will be incoming truth that you will not understand. That which is God Truth opens itself to everyone according to each person's understanding. Team up with truth; hold it inviolate within your mind; use it with great energy. Team up, masters, for the time grows near when much will be required of you. Team up to renew your own partnership with God. Team up with the vows of your entering truth — that you will keep close to truth and put it into your living. Then wait to hear that your Source has much good to give you. Team up with all that God IS. As you do this, you will bring everything that is open to good into being.

No entity will understand perfectly what is said here, perhaps, but that which is given will be reexplained to you when you need it. That is one of our functions, to help masters enter into truth and understand it perfectly.

The time is now coming for you to take control of the earth situation. There is no way to regulate what you read or what you do each moment, but when you turn to your Partner each day, you will be kept very close to God Truth that will hold you firmly in the Light. Therefore, do not fear anything. There is nothing in the world which can undermine what we have here. There is nothing in the world that will team up to bring you trouble. That which is truth is now your barrier against any incoming corruption, and there will be no way you can ever slide back into the person you once were before you committed yourself to truth.

Needs that you may have — such as fellowship with others who work as you do with truth — will be teamed up with answering help. The writer of these books has opened herself to nothing except truth since this project began. This entity was one who read voraciously everything she could find about truth. She absorbed it all, but she found no permanent peace, no permanent answers. The truth was what she sought, even as she does today.

But she often feels lonely because there is no earth person to share with to the point where she is now. This kind of sharing might be considered presumptuous on her part if others did not understand truth completely. She is advised to remove herself from other books that appear to be interesting in their psychic value. This way she builds her own body of truth — that which only her own soul wants and needs.

Now we recommend the same to you, masters of greatness. To become a repository of every thought produced by earth thinkers is to hold earth truth as well as God Truth. Which will it be — the best of earth truth or the entire open channel which pours out God-mind truth? Each master surely knows what his answer must be. Team up with God, with your Partner who now enters only that truth that you can use with the greatness of the Partner's own power!

In this way, you prepare yourself for the New Age. Use the resources of truth within your being. Then God Truth will manifest into the plane of earth as that pure and good substance that will create earth bounty.

Giving Away Generous Substance

11

Truth governs the planet, not mankind's materialism.

To understand the substance we speak of, focus on what you think you already know. Consider the earth plane and whatever you deem substance. Soil is substance, is it not? Trees, rock, metals in the earth, the very elements that give mankind opportunities to project new compounds are substance.

The substance — or matter — we speak of is part of earth, part of the planet. Mankind has accepted it as his birthright, isn't that right? Eternalizations of matter in the earth plane show that mankind takes whatever he wants, uses it, but often has no idea of replenishment. Whenever he does consider such things, he shrugs and teams up with the thought that the earth will end one day, so what does it matter what he does with the substance.

However, we ask you now to view substance from the eternal truth perspective which will turn your thoughts toward spirit, not only toward material. Consideration of substance as material has made earth what it has become today — depleted of its energy, corrupted by wanton taking and very little giving.

You must open to God's beckoning thought — the earth plane is yours to use, yours to make bloom, yours to protect with your being. Never take lightly what God gives, and never turn these earth gifts of substances into that which serves selfish desires.

Actually, earth substance is that which God has expanded into creative energy which has stabilized in the earth environment. By considering substance in a spiritual approach, you can understand that truth governs the planet and not mankind's materialism. By using this understanding, you will realize that the earth in the New Age has no need to invent earth moving machines. There will be no need to recreate what this civilization considers absolutely necessary to bring substance into submission. It is already under your control through the power of thought. This eternalization opens all substance to the control of man.

No, man does not have to force his will upon the earth substance by the sweat of his brow or by working with machines. The earth responds because it is the creative substance that God has instated with truth. Because man has lost this understanding, he has worked the substance by the sweat of his brow.

When the planet was less dense, less teamed up with gravity and with the ego structure of mankind, those who lived upon the earth understood the power of thought. Those mysterious formations throughout the world are more easily explained when man understands that thought is the most powerful force in the world. But mankind today might laugh at such a notion. But yet they cannot explain the strange formations, can they? How did man get those heavy stones in place at Stonehenge? How did the pyramids get built? How did the people in the lost Indian tribes move their rock formations which today cause wonderment?

That which is earth is instated with spirit, masters of greatness, but that spirit is thought of in the same way as the lost Indian tribes. Once they were forces to be reckoned with, but man called the work with spirit and the lost tribes evidence of a time of unenlightenment — the opposite of "progress." The Truth of God was invested within the earth because God IS all that is good, all that is powerful, all that relates to earth and man as the betterment of whatever is. That statement may be hard for some to understand, but for you, masters of greatness, it is entirely understood.

No amount of rationalization can remove what is. No manner of explanations can suffice to answer the unanswerable, no matter how many "learned" opinions come forth. The truth is the ultimate measure of the earth's goodness! But when truth goes unheeded or is trampled underfoot by those who rationalize, then the earth and people suffer. Earth mind builds its forces, and more and more people begin to believe with their minds and their hearts that rationalization is the King of the Universe.

Use truth, masters of greatness, whenever you want to open to new thought or open to deeds. Turn to the truth that God has placed in the earth, turn to the greatness that manifests when you call it forth. Here is the message of this book — that you will enact truth every day in the earth and in yourself and in those around you. Team up wholly with truth. Hold out your mind to nothing else. Team up with the Brotherhood and allow the partnership with God to flourish.

Be generous with what you understand, for as you give, so will the truth team up with more and more people. Thus the land will prosper and team up with tender alliances with that spirit which is God, that truth which is goodness. Team up without reflection upon what earth mind says or does not say. Hold wonder in your mind because what you now enact will appear at the beginning to be the "miracle" you read of in the Bible. But what we speak of is not the sometime miracle of Bible accounts. No, it is the entirely common event of people who totally team up with truth.

Resist not what is given you. Open to it as a flower opens to the bees. Resist not the thought that even now penetrates your inner self that the world around you is indeed the beautiful place that you want it to be. Hold the truth like a gem that will give beauty to those who view it. This gem is precious beyond price; this gem presents its radiance upon all who open their eyes. That is the way with truth, masters. The God-mind truth is not hard to pull forth when you abandon the rational earth-mind truth that is promoted all across the land.

The writer has not entirely given up on the rational truth because she still reads material which opens her mind to those rationalizations. She enters into such reading because it seems close to what she reads here, but there is that subtle and terrible difference. The earth truth offers itself to you for your trial and error approach. Those who work well with it give their stories, but they often relate trials and tribulations concerning what they try to do. It all sounds so much like God Truth that even the writer is offered inducements to use it!

But she is encouraged by this Brotherhood and her good friend here in this plane to hold to the mark. Better truth than God Truth will not be forthcoming, and her time must be spent developing her spirit to tune in completely to God Truth.

Momentarily I was stunned when my own experience came into the chapter. They are correct, of course. I am attracted to all kinds of positive literature that is generally mind opening. But what they say is true. I read about psychic events, and I am impressed. There are wonderful stories of people who have experienced another dimension. I just read a magazine full of interesting articles and stories. But when I spoke of joining such and such an organization and getting their monthly publication, the Brotherhood's advice warned me that getting my own truth through God Mind was one thing, and getting my truth from a variety of sources was another.

Pure Truth — what more could I want? Pure God-mind truth! I have no condemnation toward the organizations nor the publications. They probably help people with closed minds to open them, to let in some light, and to help them to search for truth.

If the writer had no plan such as writing these books, she would have the luxury of comparing one thing with another. But as it is with you, masters of greatness, the truth that you build inside you takes your time and your concentration. There is no time for other partnerships, other truth studies that would lead you on far journeys.

Now team up with this Brotherhood to open your mind still further. The wending truth of your spirit is now in our focus. Open your mind / soul to our perusal. Then we can help you with what you must do to complete your preparation.

Tone your own being to our being to receive the open truth that you must have within you to enter into the New Age with what we call "peterstet truth."[1] Give whatever comes to you as truth with utmost generosity, masters, for generosity is the way of God. Team up with this generosity until there is nothing you would withhold if asked to give. There is no open truth that you would want to hide in a closet, for closets never get the light. Therefore, always hold truth into the open places where all people may see. Then, when they see, they will ask you to share it.

Hold yourself open in this way to team up with all who want to understand truth. Team up with all who open to truth in this way. Team up with them to hold open the wisdom that God gives you. But stick to giving the truth, not to giving opinions about their lives, their earth truth nor their eternal truth. Yours is not the role of judge, jury or lawyer. No, you are only the generous giver who enters with the truth that can be used with persuasion. No one expects you to act for others — except those certain others. No one expects you to become the total mentor! No, you are the one who rises early in the morning to present what you have in the way of understanding to those who want to gain what you have.

Now, before the sun sets today, give your truth with generosity to someone else. Team up with anyone who opens to you to bring your understanding. Then, without any personal teamwork on your part that insists on opening the door that others may witness you at work in their lives, give the truth that has been given you. Then step into the next room, so to speak, to let the individual work. This method is much better than being the master in the sense of building adoration for yourself. No master may work as the venerated wise man without losing effectiveness.

Work with generosity. Work with truth only, not opinions. Work in the light and not in the dark. Those are the guidelines we bring to you. The work of masters goes forth on wings of truth, on wings of teamwork that is underway even now. You never go forth alone to give truth. The Brotherhood never leaves you without help. The God-mind connection always stays open, night and day. Enter into your work knowing you have the surrounding helpers always with you as well as that wonderful Source of Wisdom, the God of the Universe.

Eternalizations now rise within you of how to work in the New Age. Be alert to various ways you can begin now to hold open the eternalizations of truth to those who inquire. This beginning, this entry into the ways of giving truth will help you, masters of greatness, for you will gather strength as you present truth. Your strength will multiply itself to give you all that you need to realize your potential in this work and in your life.

Now go to work. Enter into alliances that will open to you. Eternalize the truth and open it to all who seek answers. This commitment on your part is a big step to reaching your own goals.

[1] See glossary.

Tender Presences at Work

12

Each master meets a tender presence who will help to manifest truth into the earth plane.

When the earth reaches its stability in the New Age, you will be met by a multitude of helping spirits whom you can count on to help you reach perfect understanding as you work with the open truth. These tender presences even now prepare themselves so that they will team up with you to be all that you need and hope for.

These very tender presences eternalize all that is pure and good, and they arrive to work with those who lead others. Therefore, know that you are never alone! You will work under new conditions, and travail will exist until there is acceptance and understanding about the New Age. Meanwhile, these very tender presences will team up with you and be the stability that is not yet present among those you lead.

Those who will work with you have their assignments well in mind even now. They have been among the Brotherhood of God preparing for special assignment. They will give you their best understanding when the time comes, and you, who may be momentarily uneasy, will have the certainty of the presences who will stand with you in all things. These spirits who come to work will be seen by many who have eyes to see. They will be as shadows to many — shadows of other people, another dimension as they might say. These who will urge you into action will know exactly how to work with you.

These presences have much to do to enable you to work in the outer plane, but they are even now preparing themselves by working with those who now open to them. Therefore, we urge you now to open yourselves to this concept, this reality. Those of you who are ready may now stand forth to receive this working alliance.

Team up now with the Brotherhood who will bring the entity who wants to work with you. This presence knows how to enter into working eternalizations and will teach you how this is done. Those who ready themselves to be your helpers now wait for your call, your willingness to work with them. Therefore, hold forth your mind into the place where we meet together. Watch the door of your temple to open as the presence arrives. Watch!

The Brotherhood paused, and I focused on the double wood doors, ornately carved and gleaming, that open readily to welcome visitors into my temple, this place the Brotherhood and I built so long ago.[1] *Through those doors came a flowering presence whom I knew in her last lifetime — not so long ago. Her smile gave her identity away, and though she is no longer my friend Felice, she is my friend and fellow spirit in truth. I say a flowering presence because this spirit is in the midst of beautiful flowering — growing, I suppose the Brotherhood would say.*

The chapter continued.

The writer has made the open contact; the presence has been welcomed, not only as the one who will work closely with her now, but the one who elevates truth into the marketplace of life. The writer does indeed sense this flowering presence and recognizes her smile and her laugh that identifies her total enjoyment of her work.

The presences must all be in place now. Each master

of greatness has greeted the presence who is to work with her or with him. Everyone has exchanged warm hello's and in some cases, like the writer's, there will be a greeting between old friends. But remember, even though you knew this presence in his or her last lifetime, this is no reunion to talk over old times! No, now you go to work.

The one who has entered, your warm and tender presence, wants to communicate with you. Hold out your best thought to this one, your thought about how you want to work in the earth plane even now to bring truth into the current stream. Then wait while the presence holds this thought to the light and examines it for any teamwork that is flawed. Then wait again while the thought is given back to you tenderly arranged to produce better understanding.

"Enter the thought," my friend said.

I presented my fullest thought of what I want to accomplish in the earth plane. I waited, concentrating on the temple itself, heeding no other thoughts that wanted my attention. Moments later the thought returned, much simplified. What I had understood to be a work of complicated magnitude was reduced to four words that reached perfectly into my understanding.

The Brotherhood then resumed the chapter.

Eternalize this new picture, this thought, this wonderful idea that your tender presence has worked through for you. Eternalize it within you that you may use it and put it to work immediately. Now you see how easily the work is done, how easily the presence and you will work together!

Team up with this presence to open your idea to earth, to the physical plane where you will instate the thought into earth substance according to the ways of truth. Hold up your eternalization to the Light and pour that Light upon it. Then go to work.

The teamwork that exists enters into your eternalizations as the help that makes the difference between success and failure, right? Remember to include this presence, to team up with this presence, to honor the arrangement we have made that you will not work alone. Team up!

Tenderness is the quality we want you to experience with this presence because you who are masters of greatness need this quality to help you endure the turmoil entering the earth plane. That which is your earth self — the body — wants to enter into the feeling nature of its kind. Therefore, each presence has, within its very center, that quality of tenderness that will envelop you and help you find inner peacefulness.

This tenderness that each presence has is the manifestation of the God gift itself, and therefore, is that gift or God quality in motion. The presence comes to you with the perfect gift entwined within it, tenderness which is a manifestation of God. Yes, God is that tenderness, but though this is so, many in the earth plane require another person to bestow tenderness. We observe this need and know that in the New Age you masters will want an earthly friend. But finding the perfect person will be difficult, if not impossible, for you must be the one who leads, not the one who follows. Therefore, you will often stand apart to renew your own resources. But when you have need of a perfect friend, turn to this presence whose tenderness is complete.

The writer has a certain wonderment at what we say. Though she is one who needs tenderness, she thinks that perhaps it is not right to find this tenderness apart from God. But she plays an old story here, one that speaks of a jealous God. The God of the Universe is that which is good, perfect, limitless, and above all, tender. Would such a God want you to suffer or to have unfulfilled longings?

Take what the tender presence brings — help in putting truth into the earth plane and tenderness that you long to have expressed to your being. These presences, remember, come to you prepared to help you with the work of the New Age, but you must realize by now that your work is already begun. That which you must do goes into action now, not later. That which is required of you — your perfect teamwork — is now to be enacted.

To rid yourself of any thoughts of discouragement that may try to pour themselves upon your truth, avoid teaming up with others who have not entered into the truth presented here. Those who want to take your truth and twist it do not enter into Pure Truth, remember. Though they are truly entwined with what they hope to be truth, they tend to criticize those who do not enter into exactly what they have.

Put yourself into your temple. Work with those who can help you gather the strength to pursue truth in the face of earthly events and in the face of those who scoff. The earthly presence we have sent will be near you to work with you in your plane where the optimum energy will flow. That assurance is our promise to you, masters of greatness, the promise which will sustain you throughout the events that are to come.

Now underline the next part because it is even more important than the promise we have made you about the tender presence who has come to be with you. Yes, the truth stands forth here as most important, as always. **This truth is, no teammate who has entered into partnership with me will be forgotten or given up for lost. I am that which keeps promises. I am that which teams up with you to help you hold fast to the Truth.**

Be entirely open with the Partner; be open and truthful. Enter wholeheartedly into whatever opens to you. Team up with that which offers you eternal peace, partnership with the God of the Universe. The work we in the Brotherhood do is only that reflection of the Partner, the Teammate who wants above all else to put eternal truth into the earth plane.

Gentle opinions will be given you to give you some one else's truth, but do not accept these words. They will distract you, provide you with words that, while they might sound good, will take you to far places and leave you without resources. The only way to go through the entering age is by holding to God Truth. Team up with God Truth and hold it within you to be the teamwork that will make the New Age ride the waves of hope, optimism and the reality of God.

Very tender presences, masters of greatness, hold the key to resisting other forces of earth-mind truth that still abound. These presences will team up with every good and precious God Truth and help you to store it within you where neither rust nor moth can corrupt it. The tender presence will not stand without great optimum energy! No, that tender presence will be filled with what is entered into it by God Who wants the truth of the eternal wisdom to prevail.

Now activate your best endeavors to open yourselves to whatever is teamed up within your being. The tender presence will be your perfect friend, the one with whom you can talk and share, the one with whom you can work. Team up with this presence that your spirit will know fulfillment and never need to seek what may be inferior companionship.

[1]"The Truth That Goes Unclaimed," Chapter 3, pp. 23 - 34; 1987; Jean K. Foster. **TeamUp,** Warrensburg, Missouri.

Open the Reservoir Now

13

Why wait for the polar point to change?
Use the wonderful reservoir
of truth now.

Now is the time to work toward a partnership with all that God pours out in the way of truth. Do not wait until later when the New Age has arrived because you want to be prepared to readily appropriate truth. You want to be able to use it instantaneously, not cautiously or hesitantly. Therefore, we call upon you right now to work with your tender presence until you can use truth as it is meant to be used — instated within the earth plane as that which is seen, used, beautiful.

To do this work successfully, you will need practice. Enter now into the partnership which is you and God. Hold this opportunity within you as that which it is — the teamwork that will bring truth right into the earth plane as substance. This manifestation must begin now, if it hasn't already. Therefore, we encourage you to proceed.

To begin, hold the partnership within you — the concept, the actuality, the meaning, the templing of you and the God of the Universe. When you have held this until you **know** with certainty that God is indeed your Partner and that there is, between you, the mutual trust and the understanding needed to produce greatness, then step toward the first goal.

An interruption put this chapter on hold for a day and a half. When I called the above material to the screen of my word processor once again, I had a truth experience to report.

No lives depended on the outcome of my work with truth, but the experience was a valuable lesson for me. I had taken my husband to the golf course where he was participating in a tournament. The tournament was delayed because of a rain and electrical storm. While I sat in the car waiting for my husband who was learning the status quo of tee-off times, I questioned my tender presence if it was possible to move the storm.

The answer surprised me.

"First, diffuse the violence." Bolts of lightning stabbed the earth, and sound waves from the thunder shook the area. Our dogs, who waited in the car with me, panted and wriggled as close to me as possible, wanting my touch and verbal reassurance.

And how was I to diffuse the violence? I was told to team up with the optimum energy which is behind the storm — the truth that "the earth must respond to perfection." Since violence is not perfection, I was told to think "tenderness" into the storm.

I kept repeating this exercise, for God power multiplied the tenderness over and over again. I used truth and my Partner powerfully teamed it up with the situation at hand. The electrical energy of the storm lessened almost immediately and did not return.

The Brotherhood commented upon this happening.

The writer put her own experience into this chapter to show that she is on the move with the use of truth in the earth plane. That no lives were involved is unimportant. When the New Age comes, there will be lives at stake. The idea now is to learn how to use truth immediately, easily and with total understanding. The writer explained that she first thought to move the storm — an act of great power and not truly teamed up with truth. Her tender presence pointed out that the electrical energy of the storm, which had become violent, could be diffused according to truth principles.

Therefore, the writer acted in accordance with the principles of truth, and her Partner did the powerful energizing of that truth. Here is how it works. The individual — you, the masters — team up with your tender presences who will help you think along the patterns that will enable you to use truth properly. This entity will help you find the orderly progression of thoughts that will infuse the situation, condition, or whatever. Then enter that thought as recommended, and watch truth work!

That which now enters the universe to be used is not pie in the sky! It is reality. To use truth you must be absolutely convinced of its teamwork with the earth plane conditions. To be effective, you must let your tender presence help you until you become proficient. Team up with this presence often, letting truth go to work in many, many situations so that you will grow in your own open understanding.

There is no other truth like the truth that we tell of here. There is no other truth like the eternal and personal truth that will team up with earth power to create the good, the pure, the potential.

To practice with truth is essential. To open yourself to the work involved with truth is what you must now be about. That which awaits you is now yours to eternalize, and to be the true master you must overcome hesitation, wonderment and the prudence of one who is unsure. That which enters to be done wherever you are is your assignment. The storm situation was one for the writer. There will be others as she recognizes them.

To recognize situations, we mean that most people, even some masters, do not see the circumstances that call for truth. But as you pour yourself into the truth, you will more and more understand your role.

Never think that there are times when you should not act for fear of losing your power. You have no power to begin with that is totally yours! You have nothing that anyone else cannot have! That which marks the master is the total commitment, plus the study, plus the work that is done with truth. Therefore, think not to lose anything! Experiment! Take hold and open to your tender presence who is there to help you be one who uses truth with abundant and extravagant optimum energy.

Bring your open mind to our work place where we will help you with your progress in the use of truth in the earth plane. We now link you with the ultimate eternalization in the universal intelligence — that which is Pure God, Pure Energy. This noble gift is not easy to verbalize, not easy to paint before your eyes. Therefore, we invite you into the work place where we will experience Pure God.

Veins of pure gold stretch out their truth to you. These veins have power vibrating within them, and we — you the master, and we in the Brotherhood along with your tender presence — go to team up with these veins. They hold every so-called secret in the universe — truth that has never been heard, principles that have never been opened to mankind, the very essence of powerful energy. Very soon you will be enveloped in the veins of gold, for you now stand in the place where the universe is held together, where the universe gets its orders, its understanding. There you will find what you need whenever there is no experience or understanding in your mind to cover the situation. There, among the veins of gold, is the center of universal intelligence.

Now you know there are resources beyond your wildest expectations, masters. Now you know the true source of wisdom to which you can go when all else seems unattainable or impossible. There, with your tender presence, you will seek that Source which will open the secrets of the universe to your listening ear, your powerful intuition, your tone which receives impulses of information. Team up with this place in your mind. This is not a dream or a fantasy, masters. This is the ultimate of ultimates, the vastness of truth there for you who may tap into that understanding.

The writer wonders if masters go here only in emergencies. This place of greatness that holds the center of the universal intelligence is not hidden nor is it forbidden. It is there to be used, and you may be the user who learns what must be known in order to be a good master of greatness.

Now invest time and understanding in what has been told you, for to be fully entered into the vast network of good that will be going forth, you need all resources possible. Therefore, sit back now with your mind in ready anticipation to realize the potential that you have to express greatness.

Work quietly, work openly. Though there is no need to discuss what you do, there is every need to put the truth in evidence. Those who note the changes will express them. You who have initiated the truth and called it forth will quietly work on. There is much rational thought in the earth plane, and when you practice truth, there will be many who try to explain it all in terms of rationalization. But if you work quietly, there will be no need for anyone to hold the truth to their own level.

Now enter into the greatness that needs expressing around you. Team up with what the earth needs, what mankind needs, what the Pure Truth wants which is to be expressed. Then enter into the daily use of truth, getting help through your tender presence who will stay nearby to help you when the time comes.

To open fully to what we tell you here, put your own life into full teamwork. Put your own entity into the Pure Truth. Examine all that you want to be in the Pure Light which is of God. Enter yourself to this examination that you become fully in charge of your own being. The master who has charge of his own truth and uses it in all aspects of his life is the same master who will be effective when the New Age appears.

The writer has opened herself to this examination, and she now works almost daily with truth to bring her life into the evidence of what her truth indicates. That she may open to this truth, we now and then team up with her to remind her of those areas of her life that need more truth. This is how it will be with you, the reader, if you submit to our doing this. The writer would not let us into her life at the beginning of our association, but now she trusts us to move in on her thoughts to help her to be the total person her truth indicates she can be.

This assessment of yourself against the backdrop of truth is needed if you are to help others do the same. The writer had entered into one truth that was not of God. This earth truth helped her for some years to accomplish a personal health goal, but eventually it failed her. Then we helped her understand how to gain complete mastery over her health goal. She must relinquish earth truth to her Partner who will then turn it into Pure Truth that will energize her being which, in turn, energizes her body. That way she meets her goals with the better, lasting truth that comes through God Mind.

Frankly, I had thought the above material was strictly between God Mind, the Brotherhood and me. But I must bow in admiration to those who write this book through me. They weave the material and my life into a perfect fabric. Though I thought to myself when they began speaking of me, "Uh oh, here we go again!" I know that it all works for the clarity of this presentation and the betterment of my own life.

The Brotherhood continued.

That which now offers itself to you, masters of greatness, is the open channel's truth that helps you appraise yourself in the way you live your life. There is a ten point quiz we wish to put to you now. Take it and record your answers. Then we will explain our method of grading it.

The quiz you are about to take has no right or wrong answers, but yet it will help you know whether or not you need to work with us in bringing more truth to bear upon your personal life.

QUIZ

1. Tender presences will help you with all decisions, but you have one in particular who is working with you. How is this relationship developing?

2. New work lies before you. What is this work?

3. Notions of your own advancement overwhelm you at times. What are these notions? How do you respond to them?

4. Better goals keep advancing themselves. What change have you noticed in your own goals?

5. Truth stands in the earth plane to testify to your understanding. What is this truth, and how does it attest to itself?

6. Through your studies you have come to accept the greater concept of God. What is that concept today?

7. Be open to our next question which is, Why do you persist in this study?

8. Other people who join you in this study may or may not make themselves known to you. If not, how can you know that what is happening to you is also happening to others?

9. Bring into the open your eternal understanding about the way the New Age will appear. Indicate any reservations you presently have about the change.

10. Better truth than you know now will overwhelm you. What will be your reaction to changing to new truth with new requirements?

— — — — —

Now we will evaluate the quiz. That which is your reality, your spirit, will team up with the tender presence who is there to work with you. Together you will evaluate your answers. Have you been able to answer the questions easily? Were there answers trembling upon your lips to be given? Were the answers there in your mind awaiting the question? If the answer is "yes," team up with the entity who awaits your gentle nod. Together you will go to the quiz to give it perceptive evaluation. The presence with whom you work will help you know what this quiz tells you about what you need to know. The results will point the way to each of you to work further with truth.

If the quiz was hard for you and the answers are nonexistent or difficult to come by, you know you need to review the material in this book. Work with your tender presence to determine which areas you need to study, which areas you must open to the teamwork. Then you will again take the quiz to ascertain what changes have come about.

This concludes our chapter. Team up to pursue whatever you must in order to bring yourself into readiness for the next chapter.

Tender Presences Come to Help

14

Many presences enter the earth plane to help you understand what may not be clear.

Tender presences enter the earth plane to team up with all who want help in putting truth into the earth. These gentle beings pause in their work here to help people receive and understand eternal and personal truth. The earth will soon enter its temporary turmoil, and they will be the reassuring presences who assist people to get in touch with their Source of Truth, the God of the Universe.

It is important that you masters know of these presences and know also what their teamwork will mean when the earth turns to its new polarity. Those who come, eventually in hordes, know just how to help each and every one who turns even half an ear toward them. Therefore, those who can be turned to hear will receive their truth, and you who know this process will cheer them on.

You only need to tell people of those who come in such vast numbers, and those in the earth plane will be reassured. That is, they will accept reassurance unless they are totally given to earth-mind truth. Those who stand by will be those helpers you can count on to open themselves to those with whom you work. Here is how you will address them: "Tender presences, those who have come to earth when we need so much help, team up with our group who has much to understand right now. The earth is not stable; we need shelter, food, clothes, protection from the elements. Bring us your help that we may use truth to bring our necessities into focus."

This is how you will address them, though you may see no one. Then address your own earth beings to tell them that God has a perfect plan for bringing them safely through the turmoil. Tell them that those whom you call "tender presences" are part of God's plan. Then turn to the tender presences. "Team up with us now. Here is Joe (or anyone you name) who is a good electrician, but he is now unable to add to our comfort. Teach him new skills, tender presence, that he may help our group in this temporary time of instability."

Then go round your group introducing each one to the others and to the tender presences. The effect here will be to make these spirits more real to those who have never considered the possibility of another plane or of spirits who can help those still on earth. This work you do is to help unite the two planes — the earth which is in such travail, and the next plane which is where the helpers reside.

Those who cling to one another and try to hold to the earth will be unsettled, and your calm words will penetrate an otherwise uncompromising earth truth mind. Therefore, do not hesitate to speak these words. Team up with us now to realize how you can add to the enabling truth that is there to be taken into each person.

Be assured that "Joe" will wonder whom you are speaking to and if there is any reality here at all. Open his eyes by saying, "Indeed, Joe, I think you will enjoy working with your tender presence who will communicate with you by way of thought. There will be a time of adjustment here while the two of you team up.

There will be great communication soon, however, and you will learn skills quickly — skills that will help this group to survive. Pay attention to this one who comes to you. I hear that presence! You hear nothing? That which I hear I have been hearing for a long, long, time, but soon you, too, will hear as I do."

In this way the reality will begin to vibrate the earth cells. Then the energy will give each person the realization that there is, indeed, a tender presence at his or her shoulder. Then they will all suddenly communicate in one way or another to learn skills that will help in this time of great need. To enter into this scene, open your mind to what it will mean to you, a master of greatness, to announce this certain source of power to those you have taken responsibility for.

Belief is a key factor in spirit communication. Therefore, with your own assurance standing forth like the beacon it is, those around you will also believe. Then, like a contagion, understanding will spread, catch hold and focus the group on help rather than on the teeming anguish of earth change. When people believe in your communication, they will begin their own communications by announcing their fears, perhaps, or the needs they want addressed. As they communicate, there will be a great influx of truth from God Mind along with understanding. Why? Because their compelling reasons for wanting help will lead them quickly to that Source of help, the God Mind itself which has the reservoir of truth.

Those presences who now wait to be called are preparing themselves by going into the earth plane to communicate with anyone who is even slightly open to the spirit and to the understanding of what teams up with them. They work under adverse conditions. They often are not heard, and they give their best and are often rebuffed. But they learn persistence, inventiveness, creative thinking. These skills will help them to be the New Age communicators who disseminate God Truth to all who will open their minds.

Those presences now preparing themselves need

people who will turn their minds to them even now, of course. Therefore, if you, who are masters, do any teaching of others, reveal the need of communication to those whom you teach. They will open their minds to these tender presences, and there will be great rewards for the entire group — those in the earth plane and those in this adjoining plane who prepare to be your helpers.

Tell others how you work with your tender presence, and urge them to open themselves to this communication that they may advance their lives into great spiritual growth. Teaming up in this way, they will be in tune with the Universal Intelligence, the Greatness that is God, the open ended truth that will pour through to help each person put the God-mind Truth into operation.

Various tones will emerge from among the gentle presences. These tones indicate that those who come to help will search for compatible spirits with whom they can best work. Because there are so many tender presences by now, there will be one for every seeking mind. Gentle presences, tender presences — we use this expression to better acquaint you with the nature of those who stream forth to greet and help you. There will be none who enter to help who have abrasive tones or critical words to speak. They who now enter to help will know exactly how to work with those with whom they team up. The individual in the earth plane only need assent to the communication and wait expectantly.

You masters already have helpers. Team up with those who come to help. Team up with their mission. Then when you speak to one person or many, give assurances that the presences are only waiting for people to open their minds. Then the presences will enter to be the tender expression of God in the life of anyone who now opens to this possibility.

God IS. Tender presences send what God IS to the open mind. Then the individual in the earth plane is turned to face the One Who is his Partner in the vastness of eternal space. The tender presence comes to help open minds wrest earth mind from their thoughts. Then, that same presence works with the individual to turn to the open channel and to God Mind Truth. We think that having an individual presence might encourage many who may otherwise not turn to the Brotherhood. The personal helper is more appealing, perhaps, to some.

Give yourself time to work through this program we have outlined here, and because you have your own personal helper, you will be able to explain that presence to others. Team up with this plan and teach it to others that we may call forth many, many more people into the work of the God-mind channel where they meet the God of the Universe. In this way when the New Age arrives, you will have more people to assist in helping others team up with what is of God and Truth.

Better understanding opens you to our greatness. Teamwork enters to hold you in place. Gentle presences work with each of you. Those who now eternalize with you send their thoughts to you that the New Age will not wait much longer. Eternalizations now appear here of the gasps of earth, the variances of the continents, the zest that wanes in many lives — too many.

Concrete thoughts of hardship and hopelessness only add to the problems. We here see the rising mists of tenderness that dissolve into the atmosphere. The waning efforts that enter as vanguards of the New Age reveal that people ready themselves for the end of the present age. There are those who work to the very end and who believe their own efforts will prevail. These, however, have no truth to help them. They, for the most part, get their strength from earth mind.

The writer reminds us of all the masters. Yes, but though there are hordes of masters, and even if you have taught others daily for the time period since your graduation, there will still be only this small group of devoted souls ready to take their understanding into the New Age. Therefore, we can see, even now, that you will have difficult days ahead. We do not minimize this period, but you know — because we have told you — that there is much help to be received. Nothing is lost, but entering truth will not do much toward alleviating the changeover from one polarity to another. Therefore, prepare for much travail.

The writer does not like what we say, but if we do not tell the truth to you, of what value are we? Though we stand ready to help, we cannot change one dot of the time when the earth goes through travail. Therefore, you will understand why we enter into your present time to explain all this to you.

Those who reach out now to accept what we say will be prepared to enter into the New Age. Those who resist what we say will team up with empty hope that things will not be as we have painted them. Putting yourself at the ready will eternalize the situation even though we cannot say when the turmoil will begin. Team up with those here who can help you, and when the time is upon you, we will then tell you that it is now. Very soon you will hear this word, we believe, for the mountains visibly shudder to tell the world that the earth is gradually teaming up with that new polarity. The eternal truth prevails, even now, upon the spirit of the earth to center on its new destination. The Law of Purity is calling to the center of the earth to respond, and there will be no denying this law.

There is no use in crying out to people to repent, masters of greatness. The act of repentance will enter no new and glorious truth that will undo the damage that millenniums of earth-mind truth have done. Therefore, warn no one, except those you teach — those whose minds are truly open. Team up with no particular time or date. The earth will enter its turmoil when the time is exactly right. That moment is written in the heavens where the eternal truth teams up with God. There is no use in raising alarms, for only those who entertain great fears will heed them. Those whom you teach must know to wait quietly, not with baited breath. They live their lives day by day, never counting, never taking the truth about the New Age to others. When it comes, all will know, and then you know what to do.

Now we leave this subject, for we know that even though you have been prepared to accept this eternal truth, the earth is dear to most of you, and the people are quietly appreciated. Therefore, you want no change. Tell no one this truth of the New Age. Keep it in your own mind so that you will step forth when the time comes, holding yourself erect and calm in the face of the entering storm.

The Subtlety of 'Let Go and Let God'

15

There is a difference between working within the teamwork and "letting go and letting God."

The might that enters when masters give up their personal power is likened to what many in the earth plane think of when they say, "Let go and let God." However, there is a difference — subtle, overlooked by many but highly significant — between what we will explain here and what people say.

Giving up personal power is not easy, for the spirit tends to explore what can be done with such authority. That which the spirit wants is what it attracts. Therefore, though personal power may become an individual goal, it is not teamed up with eternal truth, and without eternal truth there is no teamwork. To enter into the true power of God, you must work within the teamwork of the God of the Universe and those advanced spirits who counsel with you.

When people say "let go," they mean give up personal opinions and personal goals, but no one speaks of personal autonomy! The real key to gaining God power is to give up your personal autonomy. Personal power is rooted in personal autonomy, masters! Therefore, team up with the points we make here, the open truth that will explain to you the difference between "letting go and letting God" and working in the teamwork.

Teamwork is the key to power. Therefore, to work with personal autonomy is to work at odds with the best way to produce truth in the earth plane. Tender presences team up when you request their help, but if you leave them out and turn only to your own spirit, you will not gain the majesty possible. Instead, team up with those who have the understanding of what power really is.

Power is that which is written in the annals of TRUTH, that which is recorded in the eternal writings as the method to use to bring earth life into perfection. Therefore, when we give you this explanation, we only set the record straight. If you are one who quotes, "Let go and let God," then go into your inner temple where you may receive counsel. What is your eternalization? What is your intention when you speak or think these words? Where is the authority?

Teamwork, as we have said many, many times, is the key to success. But many of you think teamwork is only the means to the end. The assistance of the Brotherhood, the God of the Universe and the spirit within you who communicates IS the teamwork. That anyone might think this work you do is only a MEANS to gain eternal truth which, in turn, will be yours to use, is not on track. Therefore, we bring this explanation to straighten out any thought on this point.

That which is true, that which is totally of God is not hidden, masters. But to say you have it all within you, that you now can operate the principles without teamwork is the best example we know of standing truth on its head. Therefore, hold yourself true to the teamwork!

Team up now to recognize what we mean by personal autonomy. We tell you this that you may recognize it within your being. This is our way of showing you the truth without preaching it.

There is one master in the earth plane who now opens to truth in a most majestic way. That person knows truth, tells it abroad in the land, engenders much acclaim. Though this individual does not seek acclaim, nor does he collect money to present the truth, he is, nonetheless, being caught up with what we call the "entity of wisdom syndrome." This expression means that the individual is impressed with his being, with all that is now coming forth in the way of demonstration. That he intends good, there is no doubt. That he intends to bring the Truth of God into the earth plane is quite clear. However, he now begins to lose his power.

The power wanes one day and waxes another. The person gains confidence only to lose it. There is confusion building within him, and he wonders if there is any truth in the old idea that God is jealous of his many deeds. That thought persists until he is discontented and in a kind of fury toward God. Then his power empties itself completely, and he stands as other men, unable to move mountains or to reap the truth.

What he has done wrong, masters, is to enter into personal autonomy. He thought the teamwork was merely the means by which he would become a great power in the universe. He misunderstood or else he did not give the original teaching enough time. Open truth rains down upon him because he opens the door, not because he is the epitome of might and power! The teamwork is needed because together the truth moves. Together we bring God's power into the earth plane! Together we have strength, not alone in the realization of our own greatness.

To work with others who can help you — that is the key. The writer has been sharply brought to Light when she, at times, became carried away with her own autonomy. Though she never entirely forsakes the teamwork, she would become careless and go ahead without teaming up, without turning to those who give truth to her as an individual and as our truth-giver. This writer puts herself into the role of truth-giver without us at times, but when she sees what inferior power comes forth, she turns to us to receive that ultimate, lasting, certain and teamed-up power of God.

Those who say, "Let go and let God," often mean to be humble in their approach to God. Why? They think God wants humility! But this thought is incorrect, masters. God wants to team up with you. He does not want your humility! What good is humility? Will it make you stronger? Will it bring greater truth? No!

Humility only produces weakness! That which opens the door to God power is not weakness; it is strength. What is the evidence of strength? That evidence is entered through the teamwork, through the three who combine their spirits to bring tender truth into expression.

Now eternalize that which we bring you. Hold it before you that you may examine it thoroughly. There they are — the Brotherhood, the God-mind truth of the God of the Universe who is your Partner, and You who comes with an open mind to receive, to listen and to enter into various acts. Concentrate on this eternalization until you, whenever you work with truth, will know to use the resources that will bring great power into every manifestation!

Around sixty-five references with variations of the word "humble" are listed in Nelson's Complete Concordance of the Revised Standard Version of the Bible. Included among them is the one from Micah 6:8 that says, "He has showed you, O man, what is good; and what does the Lord require of you but to do justice, and to love kindness, and to walk humbly with your God?"

I asked for comment on this often quoted verse from Micah which many believe to be the perfect description of what religion should be. Here is that commentary:

That which is given in the Bible is not recorded accurately in that book. That which is attributed to Micah is only one person's understanding of it. The original, and we read from the tablets which now hold that material, tell us that Micah intended to give people the understanding that the law was getting out of control and that he wanted to set it straight. Therefore, he centered on the relationship between man and God, which is exactly what we tell you now. The word "humbly" had no eternalization then, and it has none now. The focus here is on the relationship, not upon the word "humbly."

That which is written in the Bible was to eternalize the greatness of God as opposed to the weakness of mankind. But we say to you, that the great God of the Universe had no eternalization of mankind as weak! What God wants is a strong, teamed up people with gentle hearts, people who give their own partnership with the Pure Truth.

That which we bring you now is not hard to prove, for there are many examples of the kind of person God wants. The entity known to you as Elijah (First and Second Kings) was not weak! What this individual did was not only reflective of his teamwork, but also of his own purposeful truth.

There were many others. There was Vatim, the oracle of the Epirus Empire under Pyrrhus, and Xavier, the truth-giver of Rome who died a martyr. Omar, the teammate who wrestled with ignorance and brought new light to the darkness is another man of teamwork. These names are unknown to you, but they represent greatness, nevertheless.

There were others, better known to you today. There was the hope of the ghetto of Warsaw, a man who helped people escape. The way to his greatness was not rooted in a one time courage. No, his ordeal teamed up with those who could help him manifest his great understanding of what was needed — escape.

Others include the one we call the Brother of Brothers, the man named Jesus who wrote in the sand what his brothers here helped lay before him. This perfect teammate exhibited the strength and might of God power, not through humility, not through weakness, not through his own inadequate strength, but through his teamed up work that entered the earth plane to create its perfection.

There are those here who want to mention many other names, but most of these will not be known to the writer or to the reader. Therefore, we only list them as our own outpouring of names of people who brought their spirits into perfect teamwork and forsook personal autonomy.

Optega, the open mind of an ancient tribe in the place known now as Canada; Imma, the child of darkness who saw with inner sight more clearly than others saw with eyes; the august personage of one named Ettebe who brought greatness into being because he understood the teamwork principle; the one named George who rode across the mountains telling people of the teamwork with God and the spirit helpers; the open minded giant named Viter who remained centered in God when the earth rumbled and shook; the gentle person of Genet who wound her hair into a coil of rope to save the condemned "witches" who opened their thoughts to God-mind. There are many, many such spirits who, in their last lifetimes, exhibited perfect teamwork. They may not be in the annals of historical notes, but they are listed here and remembered because they reached their oneness with God.

To fully understand the word "humility" is to recognize it as that which opens thought to weakness and ineffectiveness. The word we suggest, instead, is "teamwork." This suggested word has the innateness of respect, tender appreciation, the understanding of the work of spirit and the thoroughness of trust and cooperation in matters great and even matters that you deem small or insignificant. Teamwork brings you into the midst of the total energy that emanates through the God of the Universe into entities who open to that energy. This explanation is the essence of teamwork.

That which eternalizes within us on your behalf is that you open to the thought of perfect teamwork, not the abject humility that eternalizes within many. Come openly into the way that truth works. Truth that is of

God offers itself to you when you open to the work of the Brotherhood and the Teammate, the great God of the Universe. To let any lesser thought persist is to eternalize weakness. That which is Pure Truth is the essence of power, but those who enter into the teamwork will not just look at this truth, they will put it to work in the earth plane.

Those who team up with authority will send the truth to do its work, to provide that which is needed, that which is teamed up with whatever the earth plane must manifest. The person who becomes the teammate in the sense that we have described is not humble, for there is pride in him or in her, pride in the position of teammate who works with the God of the Universe to bring greatness into manifestation.

Pride has become a sour word among religionists, masters of greatness! That which opens to pride is supposed to be the very thing that separates us from God. But we tell you that those who write the religions of the world only put in the words to bring people into the eternalization of abject poverty of spirit, not the fullness of spirit. The idea of Jesus, lowly and meek, is not a true picture. Hold this idea, instead — the thought of Jesus, powerful and teamed up with the great God of the Universe. That Jesus vacated his own pride in favor of an humble spirit is not true to the portrait which he offered in his last lifetime.

How could he vacate his pride when he had to stand before throngs of people? How could he bring truth to them if he groveled or entered into self-abasement? That Jesus was lowly and meek is nonsense! Jesus, in his last lifetime experience, was the sturdy soul who wrought great events in the lives of mankind. He stood against the powerful men of his time — those who were religious leaders, those who were temporal leaders. The person of Jesus was teamed up with power! That his pride would be broken to gain his heavenly Father's favor is repulsive! The greatness of God is reflected in the wisdom of universal energy which only the strong-hearted reach out to use.

That which eternalizes before you now is your self-respect, your certain approach to the greatness which opens to you. Pride is your quality of mind that makes it possible for you to have teamwork. Without pride, you will lessen your strength and your self-confidence in participating as the part of the whole, the one in three, the eternal truth that man plus God plus the Brotherhood equal greatness manifested.

Now go forth, masters, knowing that you are the meaningful one in three who will team up with optimum energy to produce greatness here and now. There is no strength in "letting go" of your will, your pride, your teamwork. Open to what you are in reality, the One With God whose being is totally energized through the teamwork.

Manifest Your Own Truth

16

Be alert to what enters as personal, and be ready to make use of it.

Team up with the truth that will help you to move eternalizations into the earth plane at a faster rate than you may now think possible. To put the truth where it is required — that is, into the physical substance that will be needed quickly in the earth plane — you must know exactly how to proceed. This chapter is to help you put the theories into practical everyday use. But to get to this point, you must operate with the positive authority of a teammate who knows exactly what he or she is doing.

To begin this effort, we want you to take yourself in hand as the totally committed teammate who no longer hangs back in humility or in lost pride. Stand forth with the authority of the earthly king who knows just what he must do to bring his kingdom into greatness. This king — if he is wise — does not rely only on his own thoughts, his own experience, his own wisdom. He depends on those who surround him — those who have their greatness well established. Therefore, you, like this imaginary king of whom we speak, must stand forth as our teammate, one who depends upon our teamwork to bring the kingdom of truth into the earth plane.

Begin by holding court to bring the truth to your own being. Eternal truth — that which is the spiritual law — pours forth, of course, but not only eternal truth. The truth of your own being also pours into the earth plane. To invite all truth, use the teamwork. What is eternal is sure to be what other masters, too, will work upon. But personal truth is always somewhat different from what others receive. However, what is personal is also important to your work as master.

Why would personal truth be important to others? Because it speaks of need. It speaks of present circumstances. Personal truth gently reminds you that a lifetime experience need not be harsh or rendered unhappy. Personal truth protects you from entering into the martyr's role in which you team up with the idea that a person must suffer for truth's sake. That there have been martyrs is a fact, but you need not assume that role. Better truth comes to alleviate all hardship, and you can team up with this truth.

Therefore, just because you now have the role of "Master of Greatness," do not overlook the personal truth that wends into your heart and into your mind. Use this truth as openly as you use eternal truth. Why hide what is possible? Entering personal truth has no open eternalization exactly like others will give. The eternalization regarding personal truth is up to you, not up to others. Therefore, use this personal truth to improve your own lifetime experience, and when others see this truth at work in the marketplace of life, they, too, will want to be able to do what you do.

By this procedure, you will attract many who might otherwise ignore what you present in the way of eternal truth. There may be no way to reach those who stand back and wait for your particular leadership. But if they see you at work on your own behalf, they will leap to open themselves to whatever you have opened to.

Personal truth is what we must now enter into with our teamwork, for those who become masters often open to eternal truth and work only with it. Perhaps they have no way to relate to the personal truth that insists that their lives improve. "What is for me must surely be for all," they may think. "My truth opens to me, but I must help others, not myself," they may say in their thoughts.

Actually, the truth that is personal must be produced into the outer, or physical earth plane, in order to venerate what is Pure Truth. There is no way to open to one kind of truth and to close the door to the other. Eternal truth is that which is principle and law. Personal truth is that which enters your mind through God Mind to help you live your perfect lifetime. Which is more important? Which leads to the nobler end? Which provides the earth plane with better truth?

There is no difference in importance between eternal and personal truth. To accept one is to accept the other. To use one is to need the other. To reveal to others the way to truth is to reveal both kinds of truth, for they are both God Truth. Therefore, we say to you that to provide your people with eternal truth and to neglect your personal truth is to bring only a half truth. You who are masters are not more noble if you eternalize what we call "eternal truth" rather than your personal truth. Eternalizations of truth are part of the teamwork to help people see what they may do for themselves, not to turn to what you can do for them.

Think not that you are any more uplifted before God because you are a master! The way God views entities is as the mother views her little ones — with gracious tenderness, no matter which one is brighter, no matter which one is easier to get along with. That which is of God is eternal truth, and that which is of God is the entity who turns to God for personal truth. Now do you see how it is with God Truth? Now do you see how important it is for you to eternalize your personal truth?

Those who turn to you to receive help will learn from your lips, but they will lean on you as a result. Those who understand that you receive personal truth for the living of your life will want that truth too. Then they will no longer lean on you. They will lean on the God of the Universe Who wants to claim those who turn to His teamwork to live their lives successfully.

Teaming up with your personal truth is no longer an opportunity, masters. It is your responsibility to put your truth into action into the earth plane. What are you doing now in that direction? What personal truth have you instated within the earth? What evidence have you to support this requirement that you produce your personal truth in the very earth substance that people can see, hear, touch, or recognize in some fashion?

Vast resources stand ready at your claim. Tremendous beings hold themselves ready to help you. What have you done to make use of personal truth?

Team up now to work in the direction we suggest. Give the personal truth that you hold within you to the earth plane. Give the earth the benefit of that God Truth that not only makes your own life richer and more in tune with the universal teamwork, but which also makes the earth plane better by reason of your truth expressed in this way.

I stopped the flow of material to ask the Brothers to give us some examples of how personal truth benefits the earth plane, and here is their answer.

Team up to hear the story of Teneman, the woman of Ephesus, who held her own truth within her until she was overcome by need. This entity, while in her last incarnation, was open to the teamwork and helped others instate eternal truth. But people turned to her again and again until she eternalized the truth that they could not, or would not, eternalize for themselves.

This entity held the idea that personal truth was to benefit her soul, not her lifetime experience, and therefore, she held back from expressing all of her own truth. She had thoughts of greatness that wanted expression, but instead of teaming up to do this, she held back. What happened was that people began to think of her as the woman with the power, the might, and the truth of the ages. This person did not want adulation, but it came anyway.

When she finally began to instate her own truth as a means to find rest and respite from the throng, those who pursued her wanted to know what had happened. What caused her life to improve so drastically? What new truth did she have that she might give them? It was then that she told them sadly, "I cannot give you personal truth. This kind of truth only comes to you from the everlasting Source of Power and Wisdom — the God of the Universe. When it does come, only you can activate it into the earth plane."

People wanted to know how it was done, and she explained the needed teamwork. Then those who had pursued her to help them fulfill their needs, began to seek truth on their own. And Teneman, who was the stand-in for God, became Teneman, the open channel who gave her "secrets" to everyone. No longer did she need to hide to find rest; no longer did she feel teamed up with each entity who approached her. Truth was the key, of course, truth that each individual may find through teamwork with the God of the Universe.

Put the open channel into operation, masters. Put this truth to work. Never settle on a life of eventual hardship or disease. Team up with those who stand ready to leap into action on your behalf. Then wrest the truth into open substance.

Now we will help you move out of your comfortable inner temple into the earth plane where you must live and work. The temple will be there to help you with communication and with understanding, but it must be abandoned when you take the truth to the earth plane! Do you understand? We who bring this teamwork want you to resume the life you live, but with certain modifications.

These changes are to help you eternalize your truth right now — not later. In regard to your own individual open truth — you can put it to work; you must put it to work. Now step forth! What truth will you put into the teamwork? What truth shall we work with together to put into the earth plane?

The truth that each of you must choose is personal truth that will bring your life into better tenderness. This truth, however it is expressed to you, must reflect tenderness. Team up with this truth. Restate it in words. Gentle presences come to view this thought, this truth that is your own. Bring your being into open communication. Then listen.

I spoke the words aloud that form my own personal truth regarding tenderness. Then I joined with my tender presence and listened. "Team up to know that God is what He says He IS. This thought teams up with your being, awaiting only the Partner's powerful teamwork. There is nothing to add to what you have said, nor is there anything to take away. The picture is clear. Receive your truth."

My spirit moved into the waiting arms of many presences. There were embraces; there were pleasurable exchanges of tender emotions. My needs were met, and I opened myself to the most tender expressions I have ever known. Of course my own personal truth responds to my need for tenderness expressed toward me, but the reader's need may be much different. Perhaps you are in need of ways to express tenderness or how to feel tenderness toward others. There are many aspects of truth, many eternalizations.

The chapter then continued.

Those of you who teamed up with your presence found individual truth expressed. Those of you who waited on God to act, waited in vain. Why? Because you, not God, not the tender presences, are the initiator. Be true to your goals, masters. Team up to receive.

Tenderness was the first eternalization, but now we ask you to work with a second. Personal truth affects your bodily health. Team up with whatever truth is yours in particular.

My own truth is that bodily health will be mine when I team up with the "whole God concept." I am told that anything that is whole is not broken or in need of mending. Also, whatever is whole is perfect. Therefore, as I embrace

God as whole, I will bring my body into wholeness. The expression of this concept is simplicity itself, but the enactment of this truth within my body self is far from easy! I keep seeing my body's imperfections, instead of seeing the wholeness which is God!

The Brotherhood continued with the chapter.

That which does not unfold successfully is only an eternalization of failure that persists within the minds of some. The writer puts forth the eternalization of imperfection, not perfection. That which is God is **perfect**, not imperfect; therefore, imperfection cannot be tolerated by the One Who is your Partner. Put new hope within you, new hope for your energy to enact the goal that your personal truth expresses. Enter into each truth with the strength of purpose that a teammate of God must have to bring truth into the physical earth plane.

That which now unfolds to you is the open truth that is here for all masters to use. Team up with this truth that shows you how to move beyond failures to greatness.

Put all thought into God Mind. Put Pure Truth into the working part of your mind. Then live your life accordingly. When you do this, you will open your mind to the full power of God. Here is how it works. When you take each aspect of your life and live it through the God-mind Truth, then you will establish God Truth as supreme. This truth will enact itself in your life as you move into the totality of it, as you understand how truth will affect your life.

When you hold back part of your life, preferring to live with a boot in two camps, so to speak, you will find God Truth hard to use in the earth plane. Therefore, whatever you do, whatever you plan, whatever you think on, let it be that which emanates from the Pure Truth that you gather through your God-mind connection.

Rethink the exercise we have given you. Is that which affects your bodily health in tune with God Truth, in tune with what is of spirit (the controlling force)? The way to open yourself fully at this point is to keep pencil and paper with you while you do the following exercise. Team up now, team up with those presences who can and will help you examine your life in the light of what we have brought to your attention.

Write down every decision you make during each day. Then, beside the decision, write the truth that governs your decision. Will you be able to hold to this discipline? Will you take the time and the effort to write this down?

When several days have gone by, communicate with your tender presence, and review the sheet. If there are blanks where you are to write the truth, ponder these open spaces to see if there is a truth to put there. If there is, write it in and reexamine it. If there is no truth, then examine the decision, and then you may find that you are yielding to ego or to earth truth patterns or both in these decisions. This close examination is not only helpful to find where you may be encouraging wrong thinking, but it will reinforce the need of personal truth operating in all aspects of your life.

This writer undergoes the open truth examination when she communicates with her tender presence. The presence opens her mind to mistakes, to wrong thinking, to hurtful decisions based on earth-mind truth. To think that mankind, by tradition, has many right answers is to beg the question before you. Have you used truth that comes through God-Mind to make your decisions?

Just as the writer is often surprised as the truth unfolds, you will often be surprised. There are many ways of living one's life, and tradition plus "what is expected" may result in defeat rather than victory through God Power. The writer has found this so. Without giving away her most private story, we will say that her upbringing dictates one kind of response, but God Truth indicates quite another. She wants to be a true expression of God Truth. However, when it conflicts with what society has dictated, then the open truth must win over the tradition if she (or anyone else) is to live a successful life.

To write a plus factor into your eternalizations, bring your unrestricted, unhampered truth of God into the teamwork. What you enter into will be given its greatness, for God Power reaches through to produce what you, in your understanding, have formulated in your mind.

Now go forth to do all those things that require your certain effort. We who stand ready to assist will help you through the exercise, and we will help you meet this requirement of total constancy to God Truth.

Bright Promises To Keep You Strong

17

The God of the Universe presents ten bright promises that will sustain you in the days ahead.

To enter into perfect understanding regarding your role in the New Age, we remind you that the God of the Universe is teamed up with permanent and steadfast principles. Those principles translate themselves into promises that you can hold onto with the assurance of teamwork that is beyond reproach. This chapter is devoted to these promises which form the bulwark of your strength, your purpose, your understanding.

These promises raise themselves to eternalize the personal presence of the God of the Universe, the part that reaches out to spirits in human form. They offer — to men, women and children — perfect eternalizations which they can use to bring open truth into the earth plane. These promises will undergird the spirit that requires what God has to give — positive energy, the open truth on wings of greatness, the purity of energy that flows to you through God Mind.

They enter now through the writer — ten promises that the God of the Universe underwrites. To claim each of these promises, team up with your own gentle presence who will help you to understand how the promises will work in your own life, your own situation. Those who reach out to claim the promises in this way will claim what God stands behind; they will not be left with vague or uncertain hope. These promises will bring you into your full strength as an open minded master of greatness.

This first promise is THE MAN OR WOMAN WHO TEAMS UP WITH GOD IS CERTAIN TO BRING TRUTH INTO THE EARTH PLANE. There is no uncertainty, no intended clever exception. Now claim this truth with absolute authority. Put it into your being as you would file a precious address into your book. This promise is to be read, to be mounted on the wall of your temple, to be digested into a spiritual eternalization. Now dialog with your own tender presence to get further enlightenment.

I turned to my own tender presence, and enlightenment came as surely as the truth flows whenever anyone seeks it. This presence indicated that the words seem old and familiar to me. However, I need to consider them in new depth. Also, I was told to team up with the promise both in mind and in heart, indicating that I am to use my emotions to claim the truth. There were other suggestions, also, but they are private and suited only to my own being.

That which opens to the writer is seen from the perspective of her own spirit self, not the perspective of every reader. Therefore, she must refrain from giving you her own understanding of this promise.

To claim the first promise, you must put within your being the entering perspective your own tender presence helps you to find. The words are not new! But the expectation behind the words will be a new experience for those who have not claimed the promise both in mind and in heart.

Now heed the second promise. PUTTING YOUR ENTITY INTO THE TEAMWORK IS THE WAY TO PERFECT DEMONSTRATION. Once again go to your tender presence for greater in-depth study.

My tender presence advised me that this promise is my key to greatness, but then said that I still have tendencies to go first to earth-mind truth regarding various situations in my life. It's true. Often it is my second thought — not my first — that remembers it is the spirit which rules the body and the world around me, and that to "rule" I must enter into teamwork with the Brotherhood and the God of the Universe. I pondered the question of why I still think earth-mind truth first.

"Because you open to earth truth," came the answer. "Open to God Truth instead, and you will soon forget there is any other truth of value. Team up with the truth that sustains you, the truth that comes into every situation and works it through."

To work with these promises, you must hold them up to each day's teamwork. Ask yourself, "Do I send the Truth of God into this situation, or do I depend upon earth truth that has been my only understanding in the past?" Send into your mind the only truth that will make your life zing with energy. It is the optimum energy which transforms the earth-mind "hopeless" situations into teamwork with a purpose, teamwork that wrests the truth right into the earth where you want and need it!

The third promise pours light into negative thoughts that pervade the entire earth plane. Team up to understand this eternalization of greatness. TO RESTORE PURITY TO THE EARTH PLANE, PUT YOUR PURE TRUTH INTO EARTH SUBSTANCE RIGHT NOW.

The tender presence who works with me explained that the truth which comes to me regarding tenderness, understanding, wholeness and the like, not only comes for my own benefit, but it comes through me and spills over into the earth plane to bring goodness into manifestation. Here was a new thought — that as I claim my own personal truth and work in the teamwork to bring it into manifestation, it has a residuary value for the earth plane in general.

That which enters is not wasted nor lost. Therefore, use that personal truth in the way a farmer uses his best seed. He plants it in the field that is his, but if there is more than he needs, he may extend it to his neighbor. In that way, his neighbor may enjoy the seed that otherwise would be wasted.

To think of truth as seed is not a perfect analogy, but team up with the idea that nothing must be wasted. The only way to waste truth is not to put it into manifestation. And when you do put it into manifestation, you are not the only one who benefits. Enter into this understanding!

The fourth promise concerns the active energy which sends truth into the earth plane forthwith. NEW PRESENCES WILL SURROUND YOU AND HELP YOU WHEN YOU FACE EXTRAORDINARY PROBLEMS. Therefore, you never need to feel open to failure or to great fear over your performance with truth. The situations, the problems, the new eternalizations that will be called for will emanate from those spirits trained to help. Therefore, not only will your own tender presence be with you. There will be many who will come when you call out for help. Know that no situation, no set of conditions will be enough to remove you from the stream of performing truth in the earth plane.

Team up with this fourth promise that will enable you to meet any situation, any problem or set of problems. There is nothing too hard for those tender presences who will enter to help when the extraordinary situations appear. Therefore, team up with those who hasten to your aid. Team up with experts who stand ready to assist.

Eternalize the problem as you see it, and let those who are trained team up with you to aid you with the eternalization. They will give you the truth behind the problem and team up with your eternalization to change it, if need be. Those who stand by need only your own willingness to let them help.

Now open your mind to still another aspect of these helping spirits we now eternalize. They who eternalize the open truth will give you new hope and new thoughts. When the situations tend to overwhelm you, turn immediately to those who know how to see the same situations through to a good conclusion. Never sit with folded arms and a mind heavy with problems! Enter into immediate teamwork with those who want, above all else, to ease you through the trying times.

Now gather round while we bring you the fifth promise. THE NEW AGE IS YOURS TO ENJOY. THEREFORE, KNOW THAT GOD HOLDS NOTHING BACK THAT WILL BRING YOU COMFORT. Though we have said the interim period between this age and the one to come will be one of turmoil, your eternalization should hold the thought of comforts needed to sustain good feelings. Also, you must include the very clear thought of needs that will be met with abundant generosity.

Now dialog with your tender presence about this subject, for there are some of you who must be thinking that comforts and abundance seem out of place.

I am one of those who was thinking that it seems wrong to have abundance in the wake of such turmoil. But my tender presence reminded me that though most people want to suffer for their God, the nature of God is to give, pressed down and overflowing. Therefore, to accept this promise, I must release this stern concept I still maintain regarding God. I was also told that eternalizations enter my mind, but I do nothing with them. I tend to think, "Oh, that would be nice, but I don't actually need so much good."

I want to change that perception to "How wonderful! I accept that eternalization as my own with the understanding that God is the Pure Being who meets my being and brings good into my lifetime experience."

The writer perceives the matter rightly. The proof of her truth is in the entering goodness in her lifetime experience. But when she tends to ask nothing, nothing is given. Why she does this is probably the same reason why any of you masters may not collect on the promise. You either shortchange God or you want to play the role of martyr!

Team up now to move forward to the sixth promise. This promise is not hard to present, nor is it hard to grasp. However, the teamwork that is required to move the promise into the earth plane is often overlooked because people try to work first on their own, before they work with God.

Here is the promise. THOSE WHO STEP OUT IN POWER TO USE TRUTH WORK WITH GOD WHO MEETS THEM IN THE THRESHOLD OF THEIR GENTLE BEING. Who among you would deny this promise? Most would say they have always believed it. Then why have so many of you not claimed it? Work now with your tender presence who will enter to eternalize you in tandem with God.

I reread the sixth promise. Then I waited for my tender presence to speak. "The way to improve your teamwork is to take this promise literally. Enter it into the working concept of God that you use to promote your truth. No truth is benefitted by one who goes first to his own resources and second, goes to God."

That old earth truth about doing everything we can do before turning to God erodes my own truth demonstrations. I keep thinking of God as I would think of a friend or family member. Before I would bother a fellow human being, I would do what I can to bring about a solution to a problem. But God is NOT a fellow human. God IS spirit; I AM spirit. We are one and whatever God IS, I AM. You see, I can write it down correctly. Working with the promise within my reality (spirit) is the issue.

The writer has, indeed, written it down correctly. To get her to team up with her Partner first is what we expect of her. To wrest the power of earth-mind away from you, take this promise to your heart and hold it in a tight embrace.

The seventh promise teams up with the evidence that you wish to demonstrate. Pour your teamwork into this promise to make better truth emerge into the earth plane.

THAT WHICH OPENS IN DEMONSTRATION TO THE EARTH IS EITHER THROUGH GOD TRUTH OR FROM EARTH TRUTH, BUT THE MEASURE IS TAKEN WHEN YOU HOLD IT UP TO GOD'S POW-

ERFUL GREATNESS. To realize the difference in the demonstration of God Truth and earth truth, all you need do is to use the measure God gives you — His eternal power that brings His Truth into the earth plane.

This is the way the measure works. Whatever is pure, whatever is good, whatever adds to the nourishment of the earth and its inhabitants is of God. That which demonstrates hate, poverty, disease, the overpowering problems brought about by demon worship — this is not of God, but of earth truth. Therefore, quit naming earthquakes or tornadoes or hurricanes or other earth problems "acts of God." Deal with earth truth as you must always deal with it. Diffuse its power and bring God Truth in its place.

The writer wonders about the turmoil during the interim period before the New Age enters. Is this earth truth manifest ing? Truth tells us that the power of God is perfection, and that the earth must respond to perfection. That is a law. But the law need not be terrifying and destructive if people use truth to diffuse the violence.

That which is of God is subject to God's Truth, right? Then use the truth during the New Age to resist the extremes of turmoil. Use the powerful teamwork, the resources of God, the vast energy that rises at your request to bring the truth into manifestation.

Earth truth has made this moment in history necessary — the moment when the earth turns on its axis and responds to a new polarity. But it is God Truth that prevails here to move the earth into greater purity. Therefore, though the earth must undergo change, it may undergo this change with peace.

And so it is with everything! If turbulence occurs, it is earth truth that has caused it. Wars and upheavals among nations open to earth truth, no matter what they call their effort. Those who turn to violence have no open truth. Those who think the earth truth is all that can meet their problems have no wisdom at all! The violence in the earth plane must be met with the wisdom of God Truth, not the answering earth truth which will only open to greater violence.

Therefore, keep your center in God, your Partner, your Teammate. Then the truth that emerges will surmount any earth truth problem!

The eighth promise concerns your personal self and the way you hold your own being before others. This promise, if taken at its face value, will assist you in being what you must be in the world of the New Age.

This is the promise. THAT WHICH OPENS TO YOU IN THE WAY OF TRUTH IS NOT FROM YOUR OWN BEING, BUT FROM THE TEAMWORK. This promise will release you from any responsibility or encounter with those who demand you do their bidding. Tell them there is no way you alone can open truth to demonstration, for the effort requires the teamwork principle. They who try to force you to meet their demands will want to know who the others are, and when you tell them, they will know it is truth you speak. They may still try to force you, but eventually they will perceive that teamwork requires a calm, open heart and the goodness of God at its core. Those who would try to bring force to bear will turn, instead, to uniting with the teamwork.

To become one with this promise, hold it in mind until you know how to answer those who might want to push or to impose their order or their own forceful personality upon you. Team up with the promise, too, so that you will enter into the teamwork yourself rather than try, on your own, to push truth into the earth plane. Those who forget, even momentarily, receive sharp rebuke in the form of the truth remaining where it is — in the temple of your being rather than in the earth plane where it will meet needs and bring comfort.

Your tender presence may enlighten you further on this matter.

In my own life, at this particular writing, an emotional and difficult matter needed resolving. My guidance had helped me up to this point, but I was impatient. Therefore, it was hard to wait and let the teamwork conclude the situation. For this reason, my tender presence reminded me that even though I could not see the working of the teamwork, it was still going on. "Be calm," this presence said. "There is nothing that is too hard for teamwork! Rise in thought to the eternalization you received, and hold it fast while the God of the Universe works his mighty power in this situation."

The chapter continued.

That which now abides within the eternalization of true teamwork is that which will work its way into the earth plane. Teamwork is indeed the method, and no individual power can be sufficient to produce truth in the outer or earth plane.

Now let us enter into the ninth promise that will enlist your full support in the matter of wonderful eternal truth that can be the guideposts for life. Here is the promise. ETERNAL TRUTH — THAT BODY OF GOD TRUTH THAT HOLDS LAWS AND PRINCIPLES — IS THE LAMP UNTO YOUR FEET. (Reference: Psalm 119:105) Not a penny's worth of earth truth will stand in the face of eternal truth IF you truly hold it as that lamp of truth and light.

Eternal truth is written into the Bible, yes, but not only the Bible. Eternal truth will open to you in the communication you have established. The body of this truth is too vast to be enclosed in a single book or a single addition to it. This truth is found in the writings of the open channel where there is limitless room. That law or principle that you require to live your life by is written here and will drop into your mind as you turn to that open channel.

Let us present examples. There was a person who met a problem in his life. The problem concerned how to enter into the public trust. This person wanted the trust to enable him to restore the town's economy. He turned to the open channel to establish his law or principle by which he might operate his life, and here is the response he received.

"The law establishes trust as that quality of God that can be conferred upon whoever wants it badly enough to resist temptation." The one who had sought this law realized immediately how to gain public trust. He must establish a team of fellow public servants who have put their lifetimes into the eternal truth. These people must establish checks and balances for the one seeking the position of director of the economy. Then he did as his enlightenment indicated, and the public trust was his. People feared that temptation would overcome the one to direct their economy, but when he established a good team of fellow public servants, their fears evaporated.

Perhaps another example will help. There was a woman in the land where women had no authority. This woman wanted to move men into an understanding that women were worthy of more authority, and that furthermore, women could be a great help in maintaining the land's welfare. To catch the men's attention, she asked for eternal truth, and through her open channel to God-Mind came the following principle.

Women are teamed up with men in the earth plane to bring them what they do not have the capacity to have — growth of the family and teaching of the young. Therefore, earth partners have the sanction of purpose and the demonstration of goodness in the form of children. Why refuse women in the marketplace what they obviously have in the homes of the land — authority and great productivity?

The principle was true and caused much clamor among the men. Why, indeed, had they teamed up to keep women from the authority of the marketplace? Their mothers, wives, sisters — nurturers all — were entitled to authority in the land where they were, after all, teammates of men.

Principles force people to see the obvious with new insight. Therefore, principles have much persuasive power. To work without these eternal truths is to work in a dark room with no light whatsoever. To refuse what is yours to use is to turn your back on an inheritance.

Eternal truth is there for everyone who seeks it, and it will enlighten the path of life. The decisions that must be made are better answered with appropriate eternal truth. The overwhelming temptations can be met with principles that will open minds to new insights. Therefore, hold this ninth promise close to you until you know it by memory and will remember it when you face what may seem to be overwhelming trials. That which is promised is yours without reservation, masters. Truth, like gold, is here to be spent, not to be admired.

The final promise is this. GOD IS WHAT HE IS — THE ALL IN ALL, THE WENDING TRUTH AND THE ENTERING PARTNER; THAT WHICH GOD IS — IS YOURS. To truly work this promise into the fabric of your being, you need total concentration. Think on it. God — that entering goodness, entering truth, entering Partner — is perfection, wholeness, tenderness, guiding light, powerful thrust of energy, the all in all of universal intelligence and wisdom. Think on your God concept with open understanding. Then know, when you are able, that all that this concept embraces is indeed yours.

To open your being to this final promise, throw every caution to the wind. Why practice self-restraint when it comes to teaming up with God? Enter fully into the promise and release all your inhibitions that warn you "to go easy" or "to be cautious with power." That which IS God is also yours. Believe it; team up with it; open to its total meaning; live your life in its sanctifying truth.

Now eternalize the oneness you have with God. Never let this eternalization grow dim or uncertain, for it produces the power that is evidenced in truth made manifest in the earth plane.

Be the Master — Totally

18

With every ounce of your belief and purpose, hold to what God gives you.

New truth opens to you who are now ready to receive whatever the planet must undergo. This truth hovers near you and opens to you in a stream of illumination. Never doubt that which is your perfect truth; never put any hold sign on it while you investigate whatever the truth addresses. Team up immediately with truth. Team up immediately with that open channel that brought you into this communication in the beginning.

Never hold truth lightly as if it is only expected to give you something to think about. Team up with it immediately because the power is ready to push truth into the earth plane. That which appears must be caught in your mind and immediately pushed forth into the world. That way truth manifests. But if you hesitate, let yourself team up with the thought but not the power, then you must be preparing to evaluate whether or not to take the truth. The truth, masters, **must** be taken and used, or there will be no way to put yourself in charge.

The master takes charge and steps forth boldly. The master is certain, sure of his Source and positive about action that must be taken. The master knows that he or she is the responsible initiator who will point the truth to the need that is visible in the earth plane. The visible need that masters perceive is then met by the entering truth plus the God Power that brings it into visible substance. The master's job is to unify the two planes because he is of both and understands his position.

To understand your position means that you know that your reality is spirit. This spirit is joined to the great communicator, the Brotherhood, who, in turn, aid you in bringing forth the God Truth to meet the situation. Then the Brotherhood reminds you, in counseling, how to handle earth situations, how to keep tuned to the God Power which will certainly turn truth into eternalization and into visible substance.

The ones who succeed — the successful masters — have the rightness of the gentle truth at their open hand. By this statement we mean that masters know that the entering truth is powerful. Truth will put earth substance into motion on its behalf when you team up with the God of the Universe Who is your Teammate, your Partner.

Those who team up to instate truth into the earth will move into perfect manifestation, but those who team up with the eternalization that what we say is impossible, will fail. The time is now, masters, when earth truth must be given its final notice to leave your mind. To cast even one glance at what was, that poor truth that eternalizes negative fears and negative responses, is too powerful an influence to tolerate. Therefore, cast it out; throw it to the wind of God which will blow it into the far reaches of the universe to be recycled into greater truth.

To be a master of truth that enters the earth plane as substance, you must be the total master, the totally committed one. We have mentioned all this before, you will note. But there is much more to consider when you understand that the purpose of the master is to hold fast through all situations. If you waver, truth wavers. If you hesitate, truth hesitates. If you turn to investigate further, truth simply slips away into the mists of doubt and is ineffective.

Why does so much rest on you? Because earth is the substance that is of the teamwork of guided truth. The earth opened to truth at the beginning, and spirit forms took hold of truth to open this planet to substance of great creative beauty. The life forms that finally opened to this planet came to enact truth, also. That incoming truth persisted, but those in earth form began to make up their own truth, thinking they were the ones who could generate the particles into substance. Tender presences helped to maintain the earth in its intended goodness, but eventually the earth forms teamed up to posture and to dance about with the truth of their own creation.

To recover from wrong thinking is what the New Age is all about. Those who have committed themselves to be masters now take on the responsibility that those wonderful spirits took on in the beginning of earth formation. Masters must respond totally to eternal truth with no concern for earth truth. Masters must recognize God Truth, turn from earth truth, team up with the Teammate, and hold fast to the method we give you of working with truth to bring it into the earth plane.

Now open yourself to the greatness which God enters to your being. That which you are is that which is centered within God Himself. How is it possible? By turning only toward the Partner, the Teammate, to receive truth. Then you will be the centered one of whom it may be said, "This one is the total master, the hand of God who now manifests truth in the earth plane."

Behold the time of the teamwork! Behold the time of truth in action! Behold the time of energy pouring through you to the earth. Put no thought on why or how or when or the other questions for which mankind tends to seek answers. That which you are is the true master of greatness, and you are not tuned in to earth truth. Your ears are deaf to the earth truth that still prevails; your eyes are blind to the earth truth that works to some advantage before it dwindles and succumbs. The whole of you is no longer in tune with the earth truth, and your being and your body, too, refuse to enjoy that which emanates through earth truth. The total selfhood, that spirit and that body, now attune themselves to the truth that is of God, the wholeness, the perfection, the return of goodness manifesting, the entering purity, the everlasting energy that is open to teamwork, the purpose of which is a gentle returning to what is generous and what is given to your understanding.

To enter the tender teamwork that provides the earth with truth, you only need to open your mind to it. There is no great wrenching turmoil over adhering to God Truth. There is only the incoming truth to be manifested, the eternalizations that abound here for your mind. That which now proposes to give you whatever is needed and wanted in the way of goodness manifested is not only available, it is yours entirely. But the master must secure his being to the Source, enter into the teamwork, give his or her truth into the earth plane where it will give sustenance to everyone.

How can we emphasize enough what we say here? How can we eternalize the truth before you so you will positively **know** that you are one with God, that you are the outpouring of truth expressing in your lifetime experience, that you are a being whose growth surges forth within the teamwork? How can we put enough emphasis on your own role as master? How can we turn the truth that we bring you into the understanding that will insist on your own response in kind?

This is how. That which bothers you, if there is a bothering at all, is that you are not God. This bothers you because we keep repeating that you and God are One. But you know, in your heart, that you are the "ordinary" person whose life is being lifted far higher than you ever imagined. But there is a way we can convince you, we think.

Team up now with what we tell you. We in the Brotherhood, we among the gentle presences who help you in many, many ways, we who team up with you to bring you the truth that you want and need through the God-mind connection, we unite to give you this word. That which is God is yours for the taking. God gives freely, remember. God is that which is given. Though this seeming paradox may not be clear, it is perfectly clear in spirit. That which is given is oneself when we speak of spirit. You give of your goodness; you give generously and you thereby give generosity. The tenderness of your being unites with the beings of others, and that is a gift given out. You are both the giver and the gift. That, too, is the nature of what we call God. That perfection is given to you out of His nature. Therefore, you receive perfection! The tender affection which you long for is presented to you through God-Mind because that Mind knows your need. You receive tenderness and you know inner quiet and inner acceptance. Teaming up with the gift is teaming up with the Giver.

Now do you understand that you and God are One? Now do you understand that God is what you seek and what you receive? Eternalize that which we give you, masters, that there will be no more doubt about your being one with God. Enter no more awe over such a thing. Consider no further options about the matter. Accept fully the totality of what God IS, and rejoice that what we tell you is true.

Recent purification of the earth is the beginning of the turmoil, masters. This purification eternalized that which is to come that all may view it for themselves. Of course there are many explanations, many earth-mind truths to explain it away. But we tell you now — that which recently cleansed was the forerunner of the time to come.

Therefore, we urge you now to put yourself into the eternalization of truth in action, truth manifesting. Masters will be needed when the earth severs its point of gravity and moves to another point. Though the open truth will push through, you will help no one unless you use it to help the earth and its people.

The writer questions yet again about the polarity, but we tell the truth. That which is given as present poles will shift. But if you work to help the truth manifest, you can help this change to be gradual! Therefore, begin now inserting the truth into the earth plane. That which is God Truth must not lie dormant within you; it must stride forth to be seen and used in the earth plane.

Now use the truth we give you and heed your responsibility to earth and to the people inhabiting it. To wrest your own being into perfection, hold no needling doubts, no hesitant thoughts. Pour truth upon the earth plane. Team up with it, send it forth, receive it within your own life, give it God's own energy by the methods we have explained. Then you will begin to see much change to good. Earth responds to truth; people may be slower. But the earth itself wants truth and cries out for it.

Use the optimum energy today, masters. Hold back no longer. Trust our message, trust the truth, and above all, trust the Partner, the Teammate which is that open ended God of the Universe.

Now we turn to another point. Now we gently present the face of the gentle presence who is teamed up with you to help you understand what we say here. This one now attends to you, holds you in tight embrace that you may know perfect tenderness. Receive this one within the temple of your being. Team up to be in communication. This one now brings truth to you — truth that only you can use.

I paused, as I am sure the reader has, to open to the gentle presence who brings me truth in connection with this study. "There is much work ahead," my presence told me, "even though the present assignment is nearly finished." There was more on wholeness, more on my next assignment which is labeled "Answering Questions." Then I returned to the chapter once again.

The wending truth from your gentle presence keeps

you on the mark. This one will remain with you to help you enter fully into truth. Team up with this presence whenever questions arise, and this one who has become a specialist in your own being as expressed in this present lifetime, will enter to help you in the best way possible.

Now rest, masters. Rest in the open channel which has been widened to hold your entire being. Here you are at the entryway to all that you need — God-mind Truth, counseling and the gentle presence. Enter herein and stretch your spiritual being. This is the place of your respite where you gather strength to meet the earth plane demands. Tender presences watch over you while you rest and truth washes through you with the lightest touch you can imagine. When you feel ready to work, stride forth into the world again renewed and filled with all that will help you help others.

Use Your Partnership Today

19

By teaming up with your partnership now, you will be operational in the New Age.

Teamwork — that which the Brotherhood, the God of the Universe and YOU do together — is what we now address. Together we will bring truth into the earth plane as perfection. Together we will open that which is Pure Truth to the earth substance. But without teamwork, none of us will manifest!

Earth receives its perfection through our teamwork. People who open themselves to truth receive their eternalizations through teamwork. Tender helpers, whom you each have, aid in understanding this bright eternal truth that promises vast resources when teammates turn to one another.

But without the teamwork, each member (of the team) works alone. There may appear to be success when a mind is enlightened and turned to truth; there may appear to be success when the Brotherhood advances to help those who open to them. However, even the God of the Universe — with all purity, with all goodness and with all tenderness — cannot put the truth into manifestation without teamwork! Take this statement to heart, masters of greatness. The Truth of God needs teamwork, and that which you are now — masters — insures that the teamwork can occur.

Therefore, we in this plane speak perfect truth when we say to you in the earth plane that together we can provide the greatness needed for this planet earth. But unless you heed these words, we in this plane work in vain. The work is before us — the work of instilling truth into the hearts of people, and truth into the substance of the earth plane. The work is threefold and gently intertwined with the nature of what we all are — spirit. To be successful, we who hold God Truth as inviolate have the responsibility of working together.

The responsibility does not rest more on you than it does upon the Brotherhood! We who bring you these books know that we must work within the teamwork of those who never sleep! We realize that we have the open channel responsibility that will provide truth for anyone who seeks it. And we know, too, that it is our task to support you, in spirit, when you have problems in the earth plane. We who enter into the Brotherhood eternalize our work as constant, as totally teamed up with God Mind.

The God of the Universe never changes! This Being / Mind / Eternal Truth teams up with each and every one who turns to truth to have it expressed. Therefore, think not to persuade God that "He" must hear you, for that pronoun will not encompass that which is God. Think not to hover over a need in the protective hope that if you speak truth often enough, that truth must evidence itself. No!

Team up with the only truth in existence — God. Team up with that which is of the best and the open-ended power, for then you will be close to understanding part of God. Think not that you need to grovel to win favors; think not that you need humble yourself to be worthy. The entirety of God IS, and nothing you do or do not do will change what God IS. Therefore, waste no time on thoughts of how to win God's admiration or His own pleasure. Team up with what is —

the God of the Universe. Team up with what the Brotherhood is — those advanced spirits who stand ready to answer your teamed-up call.

That which advances the truth into the earth plane, that which produces God qualities into the very substance of earth is not you, not the Brotherhood and not even God! That which promotes purity and greatness of truth is teamwork. Therefore, open yourself **now, at this moment, at this reading**, to be the teammate who brings God Truth into the earth plane.

However hurtful the truth may be to your own personal desires, never hesitate to employ it. The time may come, you see, when you will face that choice — truth that will advance the planet and the same truth which will give your own haven its demise, perhaps. The truth is, however, that which works for good, though you may view it through shortsighted glasses, will be your assurance of what always brings a better existence.

Get the meaning of what we say into your core, for now we must begin to instill truth, not only within your mind, but also into the planet. Therefore, team up and let us begin now!

To enter into this final program of our study, begin with the truth that has been most persistent within you. Perhaps you have avoided it because it has seemed too volatile or too difficult or too exceptional to consider. But now we say to you to take this truth into your mind right now.

This truth is given you to provide you with the eternalization of the potential. To reach this potential, you must team up with us in the Brotherhood. We who work with you in the form of the gentle presences will now address the truth you are to make visible in the earth plane.

I faced the truth I have mentally wrestled with, and my own gentle presence insisted that I hand over the entire burden of thoughts that have bound me to earth truth. This gentle one wanted them all, and I piled them into arms that were full and waiting for more if I had more to give. "What will I do without those thoughts?" I asked.

"Quickly team up with God Truth that will take the place of your earth-mind truth," the presence said.

"What about those things I handed you?" I inquired.

"I will study them and keep them with me," came the answer.

Then we dealt with the God Truth I needed to manifest. First, I was urged to "team up with that truth," and it seemed that several presences were fitting it over and into my head. Then I asked how I got the power from God to put it into the earth plane, and again I "saw" a substance moving toward me, through me, and out into the world. I am assured that God Power has taken the truth and manifested it. The truth is of God, the power is of God, and the rest comes through the Brotherhood and me — true teamwork.

The chapter continues.

That which enters into perfect understanding will provide you with the truth you must take into the earth plane. That which is opening and unfolding to you enters because you — mind / spirit — team up with those who make this communication possible. Therefore, watch closely to see what enters and write it down, if need be, so that you will not lose the truth in the business of your life.

Work, masters, at using truth. Though you may be imperfect at times, nevertheless, you must work anyway to bring truth into manifestation. There will come a time, if you persist, when the truth will manifest with the speed of greatness, which is faster than the speed of light. Rein in your natural desire to look back at what you have done, to admire it or to otherwise worship what has been accomplished. To do this sort of backwards thinking is to enter into partnership with the past. There is nothing accomplished there, masters. Team up to work in the present time. There is no future either that is worth your serious contemplation. Why think of the future? Who can work in that time that is not here? Therefore, stay with the **now,** the present time / space project of teaming up with the Brotherhood and with the God of the Universe to put truth into the earth plane.

Team up with perfect truth that comes into your mind / spirit by your own invitation. Team up with those who aid you in this endeavor, those who want, as much as you want, to put truth into the earth plane. Team up with the God of the Universe, your Partner or Teammate, who now readies your perfect truth to go into the time / space project.

When we first began this project with the writer, we referred to what we were doing together as our time / space project. The writer recoiled because she thought such words were teamed up with what was not even thinkable or purposeful. But we again use this designation because the time / space project is now going forth not just into books but into the minds and hearts of all who have read, studied and practiced the God Truth that is to be put into the earth plane.

We name it time / space because it surmounts time as those in earth know it, and it also surmounts space as they know it. The time / space project surmounts both time and space to be the everlasting eternalization of God Truth that enters into people and into the planet to bring goodness into eternal worth. Or, as you might say it, to bring the truth that spends like gold.

Now this truth beams toward you with increasing frequency, with increasing demands. That which opens to you must be put into the earth plane either as substance or as the quality needed for better living. That which is truth need not be visible to the eye. It may be perceived with the heart, too!

Beings who enter the earth plane to live in earth bodies now arrive in the hundreds and thousands to help you with the task that is at hand. These beings are received into the bodies of those who release them to the advanced spirits who are teamed up with the truth that each master has studied.

Those who step forward with a suddenness of purpose must not be denied access to the teamwork, masters, for they come with an inner knowing to participate in getting new truth to help the planet. They will team up with you to enter into the vast network of spirits who work to protect the planet from any further inroads because of earth truth. These beings will step forward with the open understanding needed to point the way to all. Team up with them and help them if they seek you out.

Now enter into the work of truth. Enter into each day determined to push the truth into manifestation in some beneficial manner. There will be your helper, of course, the entire resources of the Brotherhood and the power of the great God of the Universe that will be yours to use. The truth will manifest if you persist. Therefore, do not go away heavy hearted or bound up in discouragement! Work, communicate, work again, hold truth up before you not to look at but to enact!

Given the resources at hand, you have the whole open understanding needed to work with truth, right? This effort is not to wear you down! This effort is to give you great energy, great hope for the future, great manifestation of good in your own life. The generous thought, the generous eternalization, the generous projection of truth to others will fall back upon you and you will enter into purposeful, beautiful, creative and energetic experiences.

The days grow short, but do not fear. The earth wends its pain into the universe, but do not put your thoughts into pain. The incoming truth of scientists will cause consternation in the earth, but do not put your thoughts and energy into these reports. Work night and day to bring goodness into being that the planet may turn on its axis with the gentleness of the nurse who turns the patient. Then the earth will know its greater truth and people may team up to survive.

Masters, the great truth of the universe is that God IS. Concentrate your attention on this truth whenever earth-mind truth threatens your peace. Team up with the thought that God IS, and you are whatever this great God IS. The qualities, the resources, the truth that is the ALL in ALL belongs to the one with God — YOU. That is our message.

Center, team up, open the truth to its creative purpose. That is the role of true masters. That is the entire eternalization we present to you.

I waited, but no more words came. Within came a rising emotion, a certain sadness that our time / space project was now ending. Perhaps, I thought, there might be something more? Hopefully, I waited for a response.

"No more, Truth-giver. The assignment closes here."

GLOSSARY

advanced souls — All souls (spirit entities) come to planet earth with growth plans. Those who enact these plans in their earth lives are referred to as "advanced."

agape love — There are many kinds of love. Agape refers to love that helps one another, not a love that encompasses a person with affection.

automatic writing — Although channelled writing is often referred to as "automatic writing," it is far from automatic. This kind of writing is a process the writer uses to record mind-to-mind communication between her and the Brotherhood of God. It ties into the writer's inner perception of thoughts that pour into her open mind through the open channel, her God-mind connection.

Bible — A collection of stories, history and remembrances that gives the progression of thought about God. It is a guide for living, divinely inspired, but it is not the only word of God. The word of God comes to each individual as a flow of wisdom, and the Bible — at best — is but one source of wisdom. God — a living, pulsating, vibrant energy — is the Source of Pure Truth, not a Bible — any Bible.

Brotherhood of God — Advanced spirits stay nearby in the next plane of life to enact the work of the Holy Spirit. They are the counselor, the comforter, the teacher who work with those in the earth plane who open their minds to them. These spirits are helpers who want to help people team up with the God of the Universe to receive eternal and personal truth.

channel — Anyone can be a channel through which the Mind of God pours individual and eternal truth. Also, an individual who is called a channel is only proving that there is communication possible between those in the earth plane and those in the next plane of life.

channelled writing — When mind-to-mind communication is written, it is often called channelled writing. However, all inspired writing — be it poetry, stories, essays, even music or artistic expression is to be considered channelled.

Christ — This is a concept of oneness with God. Each person can consider himself or herself the Christ in the sense of that oneness. When we acknowledge the Christ, we acknowledge our oneness with God.

evil — Here is a concept many people hold in mind to explain what they call "evil." This concept of an evil presence within a person diminishes the concept of God by keeping the individual focused on the absence of what God IS.

demonstration — Basically, demonstration is the process of producing your thought into the physical world. The success of the process is predicated upon a person's understanding and application of spiritual principles.

devil — The mover of evil within man, a concept that says man is caught between two powers, God and the evil one, or devil. No power can exist outside of God except as man gives that power. Therefore, "devil" is only a way of shifting responsibility.

earth-bound spirits — When souls — or spirits — separate from their bodies and live in the next plane of life, some cannot let go of their earth life identities. These spirits are called "earth-bound."

earth-mind — Earth-mind goes no further than man has gone. It proves its beliefs in material substance, historical data, scientific observations. Earth-mind also embraces religion as a worthy effort to reach God. But God is often demoted to that which holds society together in values, not a personal Entity Whose vastness is yet to be proved in individual lives.

energy — Innate power that rises from your truth — either God Mind or earth mind.

entity — When an individual is called an "entity," the reference is to the inner being or spirit self.

emptying (yourself) — This is a process of clearing the mind of temperamental thoughts and personal ego in order to receive God's truth. Meditation, willingness to let go of personal beliefs, and trusting your highest concept of God are examples of emptying.

eternalization — This term refers to the goal or object you visualize along with the helpers from the Brotherhood. They and you work with your God Truth to visualize what is needed, what is wanted. Then, the three in one — the Holy Spirit, the spirit of the individual and the power of the God of the Universe — produce any generous and worthy thought into earth substance.

gentle or tender presences — These spirits work within the Brotherhood / Holy Spirit to reunite your being with God Spirit. With the help of these presences, those in the earth plane can meet every need or concern with positive, perfect understanding. With their help, each person can be useful in his society and can help meet the needs of others as well as himself.

God-force — This term refers to the power of God that acts according to truth principles. This power manifests thoughts into things.

God the Father, God the Judgment, etc. — Terms which indicate the extent of the concept people have about God. Words that follow "God" indicate what it is that people believe.

God of the Universe — This designation is meant to open your concept of God to the furthest reaches of your mind. The God concept must be expanded if it is to meet your best expectations. The smaller the God concept, the smaller the expectations. Therefore, the Brotherhood tries to help each individual to open his / her mind to all that God IS.

God Mind — The unrestricted and unlimited Mind that produces a flow of wisdom that anyone can tap into is called "God Mind." This truth that flows with a steady impulse wants to connect with the individual mind / spirits who reach out to become one with the God of the Universe. In this text God-mind Truth is called "peterstet" — that which satisfies perfectly, that which never runs out of energy.

God-mind Truth — See "God Mind."

God-self — The entity or person who is teamed up with God.

God's emissary — A person who lives the Truth of God.

growth — When a person accepts truth and lives it, spiritual growth occurs. This growth is that which becomes a permanent part of the spirit self.

growth plan — Before a soul or spirit enters an infant body within the womb, that entity made a plan to achieve oneness with God. This plan, if it was true to the nature of what God IS, was a cooperative venture between the God of the Universe and the individual.

Holy Spirit — The Counselor, Comforter, Teacher which is the activity of the Holy Spirit is centered in those advanced spirits called the Brotherhood of God.

inner self — The reality of each person is the inner self or spirit / soul. This inner self has lived many lifetimes and will never die.

inner temple — To help us in our spiritual growth, it is recommended by the Brotherhood that we create within us an inner temple. This temple is a meeting place for us and the Brotherhood. It is here that we study, meditate, learn.

Jesus — The Brother of Brothers (Jesus) became the outward manifestation of the inner being who lived his life according to his growth plan. Jesus the man reflected his inner self who enacted his oneness with God.

love — This cannot be understood in human terms, for experience gives us erroneous ideas about love. Tenderness is the ultimate spiritual expression of total support and caring. Love is a servant of tenderness and bows before the ultimate expression because "love" gives and receives. Tenderness only gives.

manifestation — See "demonstration."

mind / spirit — The mind is separate from the brain. The brain is physical — material; the mind is spiritual. When the term "mind / spirit" is used, it refers to the reality within us — the soul or spirit which is capable, under any and all conditions, of connecting to all that God IS.

New Age — The time now appears on the horizon when the earth must reinstate purity into its being. When this time comes, nothing will be as it was. Those who heed the Truth of God, however, will help both planet and mankind to survive, to flourish and to live in total teamwork.

next plane of life — The earth plane is where our spirit selves — our souls — express in human form. The next plane of life interpenetrates the earth plane, and it is here that the Brotherhood of God work as the outreach of the Holy Spirit. It is also a place of coming and going — spirits leaving the earth plane and spirits preparing to re-enter life on planet earth.

open channel — The means by which the Brotherhood of God works with each individual to help bring about a God-mind connection.

partnership — When we accept truth from God and decide to live only that truth, we are in partnership with the God of the Universe. When we accept the Brotherhood of God as our Counselor, Comforter and Teacher, we are in partnership with the Holy Spirit.

peterstet truth — Personal and eternal truth from the Mind of God to the individual mind is called "peterstet" because it satisfies and enlightens each mind / spirit who receives it and uses it.

prayer — Religionists practice prayer to bring mankind into mental attunement to their God concepts. Prayer offers hope, consideration and an opportunity for reverence. Prayer is seldom thought of as communication between God and man. It is usually a ritual connecting man to a God he cannot hope to understand.

reincarnation — Living one lifetime after another as men and women, as various nationalities, as members of all races, we have an opportunity to enact our growth plan and enact our oneness with God. Reincarnation is God's plan which gives people many opportunities for spiritual growth.

religion — An organization which brings people together in churches for the purpose of worship and to turn them into good workers. Generally, religion keeps people from their individual discovery of God.

replenishment — When people draw upon the gifts of God, when they respond to God Truth, they replenish the earth and their lives with what is the nature of God.

Satan — The Old Testament personality who gives the personification of evil in many fictional stories. But Satan did not tempt people. He was the questioner who asked questions that people needed to answer in order to understand their relationship with God. Satan and the devil are not the same.

spiritual law — Any God Truth that operates within the universe as law — as that which must come about.

soul — See inner self.

teamwork — This term is the basic strength of the work of spirit, for without the teamwork of the Brotherhood / Holy Spirit and the God of the Universe, there can be no accomplishment of permanent value. Teamwork takes each one who understands its strength into the realm of the masters who can bring earth materiality from the seed of God Truth.

Team up — This is the directive to join with the God of the Universe and the Brotherhood of God.

templing — By bringing God Truth together with the inner spirit, the two are templed, or perfectly joined.

tenderness — See "love."

tension — Tension, tone and vibration are interconnected. Each person determines his spiritual tension or outreach for all that God IS. Tension determines the spiritual tone which, in turn, affects the vibration of the spirit which probes for the flow of wisdom from God Mind.

teteract truth — This earth-mind truth encourages mankind toward his potential, but then this same truth lets people down, for it does not have an extended, far-reaching and ultimate goodness within it.

thought-form — The human body is a thought-form, for it is the manifestation of that creative goodness which emanates through God. Other thought-forms are the manifested thoughts that we, with the help of the God of the Universe, bring into being.

tome — One book of a series of books which contain the Truth that God has to impart.

tone — See "tension."

truth — Anything you believe in is your own truth. Truth, as you take it within and work with it, develops the fabric of your lifetime experience. Your truth consists of powerful thoughts that become the center or focus of your mind / spirit.

vibrations — See "tension."

wetness — When the Brotherhood of God uses the word "wetness" or "wet," the words denote discouragement in its various forms. "Wet truth" is earth-mind truth that leaves an individual without hope. "Wetness" is the quality of inferior truth that never comes from the Mind of God.

Other Spiritual Growth books by Jean Foster

Box 1115, Warrensburg, MO 64093
(816) 747-3569
660

The God-Mind Connection

An account of the writer's communication with spirit counselors called The Brotherhood, this book provides instructions on finding and making your own personal God-mind connection. The first volume of a powerful trilogy, the book offers clear information on how to discover your true purpose and how to live life successfully.

ISBN 0-912949-04-X, 141 pages, $8.95

"The God-Mind Connection" is also available in a six-cassette album, 5½ hours narrated by Jean Foster, $34.95.

The Truth That Goes Unclaimed

This second book in the series outlines steps the reader may take to allow his personal God-mind connection to be a powerful force in his own life. How to clarify goals, form a greater God-image, build an Inner Temple, and experience truth are explained.

ISBN 0-912949-08-2, 174 pages, $8.95

Eternal Gold

This final book of the trilogy teaches powerful concepts and methods for bringing Good — or God — into a life experience. The reader learns that Eternal Gold is the God truth each one of us may claim and manifest in the earth plane as substance and changed conditions.

ISBN 0-912949-16-3, 143 pages, $8.95

Epilogue

What happens to us when we die? Where do we go? Will God punish us for our wrongdoings? What is heaven like? Will I join my parents or my spouse? All of these questions are answered in the fascinating stories told by departed spirits who have died and left the earth plane.

ISBN 0-912949-18-X, 173 pages, $9.95

New Earth — New Truth

In this first book of the trilogy **Truth for the New Age**, the Brotherhood of God, the outreach of the Holy Spirit, reveals — in an astonishing and candid manner — that the New Age is upon us. The Brotherhood awakens the reader to the necessity of putting God-mind truth to work now, not waiting for a time of travail.

ISBN 0-912949-29-5, 195 pages, $9.95

Masters of Greatness

Instruction started in "New Earth — New Truth" continues in the second book of the New Age trilogy. Those who accept the message of this book will be masters of greatness, not servants of their fears or their doubts, is the promise given by the Holy Spirit, the Brotherhood of God, to the reader who makes a commitment to help planet earth renew its purity.

ISBN 0-9626366-0-6, 170 pages, $9.95

Move Your Mountains

During her travels to conduct seminars and workshops and through letters from readers, people have told Jean Foster how they use God-mind principles in their daily living. These experiences form the basis for her eighth book, **Move Your Mountains**, scheduled for publication in early 1992. Contact Jean Foster, in care of **TeamUp**, if you are interested in a seminar or workshop — or if you have an experience to share for her newest book.